THE DISCONNECTS:

TRIBES, GOVERNANCE, AND POWER IN SOUTH SUDAN

MAYAK DENG ARUEI

A Note from the Publisher

The publisher wishes to acknowledge and thank Dr Douglas H. Johnson for his invaluable help and support for Africa World Books and its mission of preserving and promoting African cultural and literary traditions and history. Dr Johnson and fellow historians have been instrumental in ensuring that African people remain connected to their past and their identity. Africa World Books is proud to carry on this mission.

© *Mayak Deng Aruei*, 2021

ISBN: 978-0-6453988-9-2 (Paperback)
978-0-6453988-8-5 (Hardcover)

Cover design, typesetting and layout : Africa World Books

DEDICATION

I dedicate this book to members of my family who lost their lives during the Sudan's long civil war, and the South Sudanese senseless civil war of 2013 and those killed in the Duk's Massacre of November 27, 2017. At the time when the country of South Sudan was picking up from many decades of war with Sudanese (north), some South Sudanese picked and chose a fight that destroyed billions of dollars in asserts, and led to lose of thousands of lives in a direct military confrontation.

DEDICATION

I dedicate this book to members of my family who lost their lives during the Sudan's long civil war, and the South Sudanese senseless civil war of 2013 and those killed in the Duk's Massacre of November 27, 2017. At the time when the country of South Sudan was picking up from many decades of war with Sudanese (north), some South Sudanese picked and chose a fight that destroyed billions of dollars in asserts, and led to lose of thousands of lives in a direct military confrontation.

CONTENTS

Chapter Three

Chapter Four

Chapter Five

Chapter Six

Chapter Seven

Chapter Eight

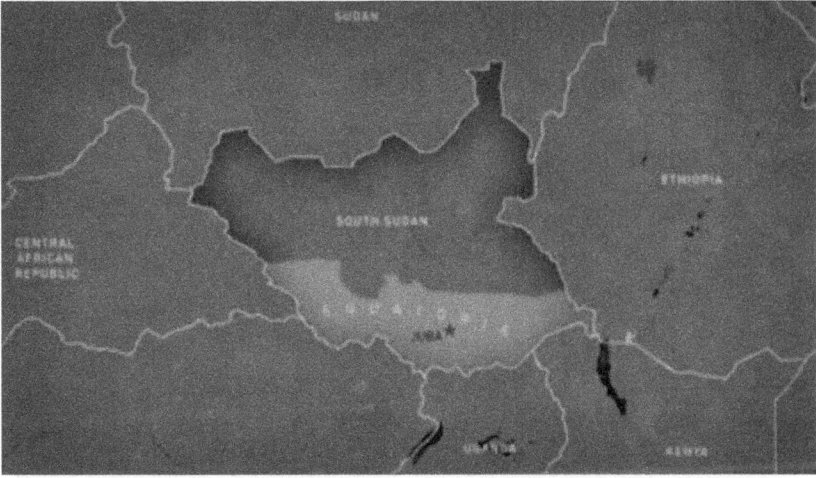

Map of South Sudan featuring 2013-crisis

Child Brides, Rumbek, South Sudan. Mayak Deng Aruei. The Shutterstock Editorial. (2017). Child Brides, Rumbek, South Sudan. https://www.shutterstock.com/editorial/image-editorial/child-brides-rumbek-south-sudan-31-jul-2017-9029312b

ACKNOWLEDGMENT

I want to thank everyone who encouraged me to put some of my political writngs into a book. It has to be acknowledged that this book started as a facebook post on October 21, 2017, and when a cousin of mine, a social media enthusiast (Machot Galuak Deng-Athoi), and who was moved by the title of what I alleged to be an article recommended turning that the article be into a book. The book explored South Sudanese long struggle into nationhood.

PREFACE

The Disconnects is an exploration of things that set people apart in South Sudan as well as across Africa. The political landscape is shaped by tribal thinking; cultural beliefs and other social barricades that create social classes among citizsens. The systems of government imported into Africa do not resonate with indigenous people's values. Tribal politics plays great roles in national politics; nation's policies, trade, investment and how leaders discharge their powers. It's not only in the government that leaders are secretly influenced by local expectations, also in religious institutions. Whenever is there disagreement in church, tribes and associates take things in their hands, and become a communal thing.

A diverse nation like the Republic of South Sudan, inhabited by 64 tribes plus one unrecognized tribe*(Koma)* is only viewed in tribal lenses. People, despite their expanded learning, and exposure to modern cultures don't always apply what they have learned to change the unseasoned way of thinking. Education is only meant for honoring, at least in the case of many South Sudanese, and many Africans in general. There is this notion of elite thinking, a very select grouping that has shown itself to have so many drawbacks.

CHAPTER ONE

Introduction
"Born Again-Prodigal Son"

South Sudanese have been through a lot of arms twistings during the two wars of the liberation struggle, and after the formation of the State of South Sudan. The South Sudan conflict is better understood in the context of the civil wars that engulfed Sudan between 1955 and 2011 (Mutanda, 2019).[1] There have been

---

1 Mutanda, D. (2019). The Centrality of Conflict Transformation in Solving Political Struggles and Political Violence in South Sudan. Strategic Review for Southern Africa, 41(1). https://lopes.idm.oclc.org/login?url=https://search.ebscohost.com/login.aspx?direct=true&db=edsgao&AN=edsgcl.602243269&site=eds-live&scope=site&custid=s8333196&groupid=main&profile=eds1

ups and downs. tribes, style of governance and power struggle created cracks and holes among the leaders. People were either pushed off the cliffs, forced to resigned or rebelled to revisit and revive their intuitive purposes. In the wake of tribalized conflicts in South Sudan, most of the enlightened youth turned into activism, and as a way to distance themselves from the biles of social illnesess. The way people entertained enthnic pride as a way to climb higher in the political arena has caused more harms than good. The aspiring leaders have tried all possible means to breakdown sociocultural and political barriers that delays progress in the developing world, but all were demurred.

South Sudan is one of the most conflicted parts of the modern world. A history of state orchestrated violence goes back to enslavement and colonization in the nineteenth and early twentieth century, which gave way to prolonged and increasingly intense post-colonial civil wars. Political unrest in the south began in 1955, the year before Sudan's independence, following a mutiny of Southern soldiers in the town of Torit.[2]

---

2   Cormack, Z. (2017). The spectacle of death: visibility and concealment at an unfinished memorial in South Sudan. Journal of Eastern African Studies, 11(1), 115–132. https://lopes.idm.oclc.org/login?url=https://search.ebscohost.com/login.aspx?direct=true&db=edb&AN=121549844&site=eds-live&scope=site&custid=s8333196&groupid=main&profile=eds1 - In the course of 50-years liberation struggle; Sudanese, and South Sudanese in particular sacrified generations for the total freedom. People who participated in the wars of liberation saw themselves are indebted to the human dignity, so they took their duties to the next level.

Hunting Corridor

Once upon a time, there was a Governor who rose through the rank of the war of liberation, became a colonel in the army and was appointed Governor. When the first ever election was held, he was denied by his party to be the flag bearer and chose to run as an independent candidate. Having done that, he won the race despite many attempts to deny him of his huge support. A female politician from his home state placed a close look of his activities, and deployed a political trap in everything he does. Nationwide, things changed, and there was a new election coming up.

The warlords turned politician flapped their wings, and in almost every major region in the country, these people who have been in military leadership for more than two decades were eyeing for the nation's highest throne. This is not some new in a nation that just emerged out of war. Like any country in Africa, incumbent President is not easy leader to be relieved from post through the supposedly democratic campaign. So, the aspirants chose a platform driven by political alliances, and which would have given them a fair political share after election. Without wasting time, the incumbent solidifieded his political based, re-energized his followers and setoff an alarm for imaginery coup attempt. The world's newest nation was set ablaze, a story of once glorified nation-state to a failed State based on fragility index. Since the war broke out in December 2013, South Sudan retained top position on the fragile States Index. Per 2021 Fragile States ranking, South Sudan was rank

4th out of the 179 countries ranked.[3] It is a very serious indication that lots more works need to be done in order for South Sudan to move forward. The level of violence in South Sudan, and political disorientation throughout the country are signs that the country is far below stability standards.

Politics and Lineage

In the practical sense, relatives in political arena become the worst woes. The South Sudanese are not in isolation; there have been many instances where relatives with opposing views have been caught camping near cliffs. Like in the Sudan where the like of Sadiq Al-Mahdi and Hassan Al-Turabi have lived an opposite lifestyle despite them being in-laws, South Sudanese neatly copied from their old guards.

During the condominium rule, families who had held authority under Turko–Egyptian rule were reinstated as part of the government bureaucracy (Raftopoulos, & Alexander, 2006, p.9).[4] On the shores of the in-law waters; there were cousins who have ever fell on opposite sides. In 1991, quite a number of SPLA officer deserted their posts, and they were followed by relatives even through they had not political agenda. The rest of

---

3   The Fund for Peace. (2021). Measuring Fragility Risk and Vulnerability in 179 Countries. Fragile States Index. https://fragilestatesindex.org/.

4   Raftopoulos, Brian, & Alexander, Karin. (2006). Peace in the Balance: The Crisis in Sudan. Journal of Eastern African Studies. Institute for Justice and Reconciliation. http://africanminds.co.za/wp-content/uploads/2012/05/Peace%20in%20the%20Balance%20-%20The%20Crisis%20in%20Sudan.pdf

his family members stood within the ranks & files of the liberation struggle, gained themselves a great respect and recognition. When things went wild, unseasoned leaders took shortcuts or unauthorized extended leaves.

A little over a year into the self-governing period, a fight over recognition made aspirants with ambiguous political agendas to make a roaring exit strategy. All things considered, everyone came to the table, there a new election and a referendum coming up. The conversation became, money was flying in the sky, and a dawn for new deal make people buddies. The odds were muted; having been branded, educated by the same uncle was the unifying substance that signify togetherness.

Well, flavor ends with the last sip; therefore, things will always go back to the initial point of departure. It will always be remembered, the veteran of the first war of liberation war would be the unifying figure; the reason he was given three days of mourning by the president of the Republic. The thirst for powers and wealth is more than a black magic. When the main source of revenue was dripping dust, new paths were sought. Imagine; making erratic political decisions faraway from the borders of the State. The podium was a distance where the speaker's couldn't not be reflected to the audiences. Him, the sneaky guy was picked up by the pack foxes after his beloved cousins reclaimed his old house despite have guided the leader of the packs. For words make life meaningful; interest kills, and people are forever divided by greed for everything.

The political history of South Sudan has followed a tortuous, though well-documented trajectory. Since achieving independence from Britain in 1956, Sudan has experienced almost continuous conflict, which has caused widespread disruption and placed considerable pressure on bordering states through demands placed on them to provide refugee assistance/ operational bases for rebel movements.[5]

To say the least, the lunatics who making living by throw dirts on bystanders took the chance, nailed their relatives on cross, and in the name of providers. Two weeks of crisscrossing on the social media was more of a bullfights and above cockfights in the prwpheries of prophetic chaos. The people who were at the prepubescent stage could not separate State's affairs from family, clan and sections's affairs. Therefore, they occupied public offices, and still operated with village's mindset. The immaturity seen in most statemen led to political pheromones, which then affected behavior of the general public as no one seemed to know the direction.

It was something expected of a country born out of fierce liberation struggle, South Sudan tenfolded poverty by its 10th year anniversary. By the end of the year 2020, there were staggering number of South Sudanese in the refugee camps and IDP camps. At the same time majority who were resettled in developed nations of the West see the second countries as homes because there is not much hope left in South Sudan. It was a everyone hope that those who fled the country during the war

---

5   Impey, A. (2013). Keeping in touch via cassette: tracing Dinka songs from cattle camp to transnational audio-letter. Journal of African Cultural Studies, 25(2), 197–210. https://lopes.idm.oclc.org/login?url=https://search.ebscohost. com/login.aspx?direct=true&db=edb&AN=87820879&site=eds-live&scope=site

would be reunified with their family members, and life would resume normally. It only exist as a biblical myth as nothing was seen forthcoming despite abundance of resources; minerals, oil reserve and arable lands throughout the country.

The Benchmark

A new country comes with challenges; international borders and communal boundaries are power-generating. "Countries are often forged in fire and blood, and it now looks inevitable that violence will attend the birth of the world's newest nation" (Ghosh, 2010).[6] The war between north and south officially came to an end, but there are outstanding issues that require the brave to push for demarcation and make a gain while saving the interest for the majoring. Once an outpost is a powerhouse; number don't lie. A democratic process was compromised in the name of creating a strong political hold, and rewarding those who stood firm in time of crisis. Well, in the bushes; all who participated in battles were revered commanding officers. Therefore, picking among them is choosing a new battle. That has to be done with possibilities of monumental rupture at play. One in, one out. A change of position means a brand new challenge.

The prime competitors exhausted their allegiance, dividends

---

6   Ghosh, B. (2010). Birth Pains. TIME Magazine, 176(13), 40–45. https://lopes.idm.oclc.org/login?url=https://search.ebscohost.com/login.aspx?direct=true&db=ulh&AN=53787753&site=eds-live&scope=site&custid=s8333196&groupid=main&profile=eds1

could not be realistically calculated. The shopping continued; a nearby village had a sticky Army General, revered fighter who could easily be counted as one of the disoriented, yet his actual base is nobody altar. When the spirit refused to take charge of the new venue, the messengers have to find the balance. The bush and the home have dissent persons who could easily be turned into hardcore loyalists, but that would means breaking the bank. The iron makers had to find the source of the agony. Anyhow trusting turned out to be too expensive. With that, loyalty to a person does not means allegiance to the nation. For the most parts, the opposite poles can be made noncompliance by nonpayment. What is the incentive for all of that? Absolutely none, but the crow has better idea why roofing must be inspected before trusting the landing. A magnet or oily space can tragically zero out the hardwork and the long awaited uncalculated moves. South Sudan's model of State formation and State building suffered gravely from what would be termed as design problems.

South Sudan emerged as an independent country before the completion of state formation process as per the European model. Many of its people still live outside the state precincts; politics have not been sufficiently emancipated from the person, or, by extension, from the ethnic community from which hails the person exercising authority.[7]

---

7   Morris, Nsamba Adam. (2011). State Building and Development in South Sudan. African Research and Resource Forum. https://www.academia.edu/26585030/State_Building_and_Development_in_South_Sudan

By the virtue of what transpired after the independence, predictions about what was thougth of independent South Sudan and post-independence observations mirrored each other. It did not come as a surprise to people who have well vested in States formatiom and State building. There is a lot more work requires of independent State than envisioned and anticipated by the founding principles. The freedomfighters committed a great deal on buddying themselves.

Loyalty Pays

When starting a journey to nowhere, faith and relentless efforts are needed. The very people who rise beyond their potential are those who sacrifice themselves for loyalty, take all the risk and selflessly serve their masters to the full. It takes many years for such vision to materialized. Once the peak has been reached, soul-searching is spearheaded. A venue of gear means a change of strategy, and mission old garden. During South Sudan's struggle for independence, people from all walks of life sought influence by skipping lines, and paying attention to long term gain rather than short term pleasures. Conflict transformation helps South Sudan in realizing that there is more to their future as a country rather than power struggles largely driven by ethnic politics (Mutanda, 2019).[8] This is not to forget that any

---

8   Mutanda, D. (2019). The Centrality of Conflict Transformation in Solving Political Struggles and Political Violence in South Sudan. Strategic Review for Southern Africa, 41(1). https://lopes.idm.oclc.org/login?url=https://search.ebscohost.com/login.aspx?direct=true&db=edsgao&AN=eds-gcl.602243269&site=eds-live&scope=site&custid=s8333196&groupid=-main&profile=eds1

path is painted with visible marks. As sun took the right angle to the dust, lots of changes happens including the vanishing of the leaders who once led the movement. The change ridged a lasting impact on next generation. The compromise between the past and the present have been to be reached.

The magnitude of the shift abruptly ended others' intelligence works and all the interwoven networks, and one a possibility of new alliance as a matter of survival. The invisible hands shafted the nobility as the information once held at a central center get distributed to all corners including the air. The sophisticated trustees where let off the hook for retirement in the home bases. Nobody, returnees always create discomforts, and re-engineer the political landscape. The streets and coffee place are packed with jobseekers, and the willing are left unempowered and politically disoriented beyond recognition. It has been repeatedly recorded that every time people in Government (s) lose their jobs, they reconcile with the majority consensus that the Government of South Sudan has not to the citizens' expectations.

Life is Itself a Devil in the Room

Halfway through the first decade of the war of liberation, some people found conform zones as their conformity to the rules have earned a stay away from the flying debris. Well, revolution is a risky business, and not all who theoretically agreed to be abided by Mission stay the whole cause. As remembered, quite a number of officers were given assignments in refugee camps

(Itang, Pagnidu and Dimma) in Ethiopia. With the quest for more influence, some shrewd decisions were made to shake the found of the liberation movement that unquestionably give instructions, and no questions asked. Such attitudes for a re-evaluation of war strategies required based and a supply route. The way getaway was Itang, so the camp manager was swayed to re-direct reliefs toward the new war zone and the major enemy of the people. The devil visited Sudanese in an unincorporated passion.

The masses who once lived in paradise were instructed to flee westward while the political fracturing was being framed. The historical 1991 split was born. The rebels signed a relief package in the name of Khartoum Peace Agreement of 1997 Some 10 years later since the split, the Sudanese Government in Khartoum dishonored their commitment to the 1997 peace and some officers had to seek a way out of the trap. In 2001, the first batch, which included the famous Itang's camp manager rejoined the people's movement, paving the way for everyone else to rejoin as dust settles. The partners stayed in touch till 2010 election caused another political rift. The cracked was sealed when election was seen as thing of the past. The nation was graciously in the hands of the former warlords, and its independence guaranteed as the world's power brokers fledged full protection under the United Nations charter.

The Unreasonable Beginning!

When South Sudanese attained self-rule in 2005, the people and the rebel-turned statemen wanted something to start with. So, having a system that is inclusive and not too hard to handle was availed. The Government of Southern Sudan was to be headed by the president. The president was empowered to appoint group of officials later known as the South Sudan council of ministers (SSCM). The SSCM was the engine to accelerate South Sudanese statehood aspiration, and to manage affairs of the region more-like a government of the Republic would do.

The president of South Sudan appointed the South Sudan Council of Ministers (SSCM) in consultation with the vice president and following approval of a simple majority of all members of the South Sudan Legislative Assembly. The president and vice president were members of the SSCM, which had a quota requiring that least 25 percent of the members should be women. The SSCM was the highest executive authority in South Sudan, and its decisions prevailed over all other executive decisions (Berry, 2015, pp. 238).[9]

No surprise, many South Sudanese, especially those in the first Government wanted to stay in a transition. The powers of the presidents remained untouched, and there was a major support from the president's base. That became the origin of

---

9   Berry, L. B. (2015). Sudan, a country study / Federal Research Division, Library of Congress; edited by LaVerle Berry. *Fifth edition.* https://permanent.fdlp.gov/gpo63176/CS_Sudan.pdf#

governance issues and led to all-out war in 2013. Quite a few things triggered the war: lack of trust and fear of political domination/isolation. This was later confirmed by the account of those who fell out with the Government. Whenever people lose their positions in Government, they come to terms with the public, and expressed their fear and the need for reforms in the Government.

For much of the interim period (2005-2011), the politicians remarried as they fought possible international isolation should they behave more like baboons in the rainy forest jungle. The carnage that took place in the run-up to the ruling party's flag-bearer spoke volumes. It is wellrecognized that new war within the ranks and files of the SPLA caused wobbles, and those who lost grip of the fairshare of the liberation were spotted footing in hot a pursuit. Well, it was an exigent situation that called for urgent response by those in power, and it was somewhat a "die-trying" to those who felt annihilated by their colleagues. As a matter of principles, and as the saying goes, "goes what goes around comes arounds", those who once championed themselves as having conquered the streets and bushes of South Sudan were seen engaging in a door-to-door manhunting. The can of power got its crucial knob loosen in late 2012, and the situation went out of hand on July 23, 2013 when the President of the Republic sacked his vice president, and letting the guns go off again.

The removal of Vice President Machar has been alternately described as a political or an ethnically-motivated event, as well as categorized as a hybrid of both issues. It is undeniable that the two men are from different ethnic groups, with Kiir belonging to the Dinka and Machar belonging to the Nuer group, but the roots of their disagreements are indisputably political. Tensions between the President and Vice President had gradually escalated for months prior to the dismissal. This was due, in part, to Machar's denunciation of the President in a televised address in which he announced himself as the leader of the SPLM/A in Opposition.[10]

People who live their political life in denial do not want to accept the narrative that led to deadliest conflict in South Sudan. The fact that vice president was dismissed from his post as the country's ruling party vice president helped mobilized the Nuers to join the war in big numbers. It has been the case throughout the centuries that this South Sudan's largest tribes would come head-to-head on battlefield. People can believe whatever they want to believe. But history will remember that ethnic uneasiness led to destructions and loss of lives in South Sudan, following dismissal of the vice president. The cycles of violence across South Sudan have seen ethnic dimensions, the conflict between Nuers and the Dinkas. Political struggles and political violence in South Sudan have significantly led to the deterioration of human security and human rights (Mutanda,

---

10 Kuntzelman, C. C. (2013). South Sudan: Solutions for Moving beyond an "Ethnic Conflict." *International Research and Review, 3(1), 81–118.* https://lopes.idm.oclc.org/login?url=https://search.ebscohost.com/login.aspx?direct=true&db=eric&AN=EJ1149924&site=eds-live&scope=-site&custid=s8333196&groupid=main&profile=eds1

2019).[11] The South Sudanese politicians who live in a grey area have been quick to dismiss that, but the fact remains that they run to their tribal bases to gather supports and stage the war behind the scenes. Even within the Dinkas or the Nuers, mini conflicts have been fought featuring sub-tribes against sub-tribes, and sub-clans against sub-clans. The only way to forge a peaceful coexistence within the South Sudan is for all the stakeholders to have open-honest discussions about causes of conflicts and put honest solutions so coming generations don't such wrong footings that have destroyed the country's aspirations.

In the first phase of the political turmoil, things got screwed up. The fighting quickly spread and soon the military divided along ethnic lines with war crimes and massacres, the targeted killing of key leaders, and worsening corruption where the government failed to hold anyone accountable (Shaffer, 2021).[12] The chaose did not end in Juba, it spreaded through out the country, and across the worldwide waves, and as supporters of disgruntled mobilize for a game-changing catchall exercise. Three years down the road, it was a of a marathon for the dis-

---

11   Mutanda, D. (2019). The Centrality of Conflict Transformation in Solving Political Struggles and Political Violence in South Sudan. Strategic Review for Southern Africa, 41(1). https://lopes.idm.oclc.org/login?url=https://search.ebscohost.com/login.aspx?direct=true&db=edsgao&AN=eds-gcl.602243269&site=eds-live&scope=site&custid=s8333196&groupid=main&profile=eds1

12   Shaffer, Ryan. 2021. "South Sudan: The Untold Story from Independence to Civil War." TERRORISM AND POLITICAL VIOLENCE 33 (7): 1581–85. doi:10.1080/09546553.2021.1976551, https://lopes.idm.oclc.org/login?url=https://search.ebscohost.com/login.aspx?direct=true&db=edswss&AN=000705040800017&site=eds-live&scope=site&custid=s8333196&groupid=main&profile=eds1

lodged and their alives across the world. Like other conflict in the continent, a peace Accord was sponsored by the regional brokers, and that did not materialized till the 2016 when peace deal was signed, and the rebels were allocated a small portion of the Government. Because chaos does not always benefits late-joiners, some splinter groups were left grasping for their lives.

A movie like scenario, later named as "dogfight" at the State House was eveidently cooked as claims turned out not to be true. While the fire burned, lots of things came into play; seizing the portion as a strategy to quell the situation and reclaim dried banks accounts. The two factions of the same evils were born, leaving one in hotel and the other one a forty-days aerial manhunt. The political struggle in South Sudan has been the real cause of all the destructions in the nation. There is this notion of best fighters and best leaders. South Sudanese have much of their deeds cropped from historical and prophetic theories whereby tribes heavily rely on their own beliefs. It has been obersved that "over the past 120 years, Nuer practices and traditions of prophecy have evolved in tandem with state-based assertions of exclusive control over the legitimate use of force and, thus, over the lawful power to kill or protect" (Hutchinson, & Pendle, 2015, p. 415).[13]

The history of political violence, and violence against civilians is voluminous. There is enormous enormous literature

---

[13]   Hutchinson, Sharon E, & Pendle, Naomi. (2015). Violence, legitimacy, and prophecy: Nuer struggles with uncertainty in South Sudan. Journal of American Ethnological Society. https://www.academia.edu/22777271/Violence_legitimacy_and_prophecy_Nuer_struggles_with_uncertainty_in_South_Sudan

squaring what political forces have done in the old Sudan and the now South Sudan. For over 5 decades, researchers have come to Sudan, mainly collect stories from the civil population, and all these have been put up by various research institutions throughout the world. Like previously recorded conflicts in the Sudan, recent civil conflicts in South Sudan have taken the shape od the historical accounts.

The impact of the civil war on the South Sudanese people has been colossal. Almost a third of the population has fled their homes, either internally or into neighboring states. Uganda now has the world's largest refugee camp, Bidi Bidi, hosting some 270,000 South Sudanese. 400,000 South Sudanese – mainly supporters of Machar – have also returned to Sudan, itself one of the world's least stable countries, from which the South Sudanese voted overwhelmingly to secede.[14]

In the world where nothing works, people would use anything to climb up the stairs: tribe, church and regionalism. This introduction is concluded by stating that South Sudanese create categories for political reasons. For example, Jieng council of elders (JCE), Nuer council of elders (NCE), Bari council of elders (BCE) and Equatoria council of elders (ECE) among others are quasi-political entities that use extended lineage to grasp and expand political spaces. This is also true with regional social clubs that have been used over the years to forge political

---

14   Taylor & Francis. Conflict and impasse in South Sudan. (2017). Strategic Comments, 23(4), i–ii. https://lopes.idm.oclc.org/login?url=https://search.ebscohost.com/login.aspx?direct=true&db=edb&AN=123226392&site=eds-live&scope=site&custid=s8333196&groupid=main&profile=eds1

alliances and cement allegiance to people's shared roots. On the religious ground, dioceses were created based on ethnicities. Religious Texts such as the Christians Bible carries tribal identities. For example, Dinka Bible society isn't a religious identification, but rather an ethnic ideological imperialism that enthnically claims ownership of the Christianity teachings.

Tribes, Governance and Power

The path to nationhood for South Sudanese was never a smooth ride. South Sudan's birth was very rocky, founded in time when the people of SUDAN have waged bloodiest wars with Kharotum based regimes. This dated back early days of colonization; the British colonial officials fostered a system of administration from the central Nile region which entailed the neglect of peripheral areas, and separated the Southern provinces of Upper Nile, Equatoria, and Bahr al Ghazal from the North. The latter were largely left to their own devices, economic and political development being concentrated along the central Nile.[15] There were a lot of ups and downs as policies annihilate black from Sudanese from rest of the country. The issue identity crisis and religious intolerance contributed to people losing their sense of self. For example, sidenotes had this say about fear and future of what would be independent South Sudan:

---

15   Berry, L. B. (2015). Sudan, a country study / Federal Research Division, Library of Congress; edited by LaVerle Berry. *Fifth edition*. https://permanent.fdlp.gov/gpo63176/CS_Sudan.pdf#

The prospect of independence has exacerbated rivalries between the south's patchwork of tribal groups and armed militias
that are also vying for control of the oil; some blame al-Bashir
for fomenting internecine conflict. Certain SPLA commanders
have turned renegade. Many southerners are alarmed that the
regional government is dominated by a single tribe, the Dinka.
"The other tribes worry that the Dinka will not share power
after independence," says Patrick Gorham, director of Africa
Writes, an NGO which studies tribal cultures. There's growing
concern that the creation of Southern Sudan will merely usher
in a new stage of an old resource war.[16]

It was self-evidenced that South Sudanese will gain their independence through ballots if granted the opportunity to decide on the referendum exercise. But, smaller tribes in South
Sudan feared largest tribes, Dinka to be specific. The liberation struggle have had its odds; South Sudanese have fought
themselves for over 50 years, and they blame have been squarely
placed on the post-colonial assumptionists. If South Sudanese
were to blame someone for the long suffering, then it would be
the British. The colonial Administration had done something
terrible to the Sudanese people, leaving South in the hands of
northern Islamists was the origin of all Sudanese cultural, social, political and religious crises.

16   Ghosh, B. (2010). Birth Pains. *TIME Magazine, 176(13),* 40–45.
https://lopes.idm.oclc.org/login?url=https://search.ebscohost.com/login.
aspx?direct=true&db=ulh&AN=53787753&site=eds-live&scope=site&-
custid=s8333196&groupid=main&profile=eds1

British authorities treated the three provinces in the South as a separate region. The colonial administration, as it consolidated its position in the 1920s, detached the South from the rest of Sudan for all practical purposes. The period's Closed Districts Ordinance barred Northern Sudanese from entering or working in the South and reinforced the separate-development policy. Moreover, the British gradually replaced Arab administrators and expelled Arab merchants, thereby severing the South's last economic contacts with the North. The colonial administration discouraged Islam and Arab customs and dress but attempted to revitalize African customs and tribal life that the slave trade had disrupted. Finally, a 1930 directive stated that blacks in the Southern provinces were to be considered as a people distinct from Northern Muslims and that the region eventually should be integrated into Britain's East Africa colonies (Berry, 2015, pp. 26).[17]

As a multiethnic, multilingual, multicultural and multireligious State, South Sudan has it shortcomings just any country in the world. For the purpose of the book, tribes, governance and power will be defined as they are the themes for this book. The most causes of social and political unrests in South Sudan are interconnected with tribes, system of government and the way leaders keep the balance. The issue of progressive and reformist thinkers will be discussed at the end of the book.

---

17   Berry, L. B. (2015). Sudan, a country study / Federal Research Division, Library of Congress; edited by LaVerle Berry. Fifth edition. https://permanent. fdlp.gov/gpo63176/CS_Sudan.pdf#

Tribes

Like any other country in Africa, South Sudan is made up of many tribes, all of which have very distinct cultures, social structures and tribal political setups. Ever since, tribes valued the institution called marriage, and they tended to put it above everything. Their societies invest in marriage as a way to procure, define, and forecast prosperity. Wealth has always been defined in the form of number of people in a tribe, clan, and sections. The most populous units were presumably the wealthiest as daughters are married off for material goods, animals and other valuables. Unlike other societies, South Sudanese communities considered their tribal and clannish lineage as so sacred, and everything that they do has much to do with local pride. With the changes that have come to the society, tribal alliance and allegiance remains unchanged. The political landscape is often shaped by how much an aspirant receive from his Base. That lead us to how a society governed and subsequence outcomes of such dealing.

The most detrimental part for living in a tribalized society is all that goes wrong when politics goes wild. After South Sudan's independence, many South Sudanese and the world at large hoped that things will shift for the better. Unfortunately, independence came with its own unique social and political problems. The nation entered into a dark age where political rivalry among the elites led to fragmentation. With discontented political manicacs having retreated to their tribal quotas, the mafias across the country took law into their own hands; citizens and their livestocks were subjected inhumane treatments, and in name of protecting tribal pride and belongings. People, through their own understanding of who they are and who they should be take their ethnic and tribal identity as a shield. The citizens are the mechanization for prosperity and nation's wellbeing. But because citizens identify them as from certain tribe instead of the state or the localities, they carry in the tongue a pride that scary off others who are not from their own tribe.

Ethnicities conceived in this way are thus sites of struggle, whether expressed in overt interor intra ethnic struggles or contested in small acts of resistance. In the Sudanese civil war the sides struggled to impose different definitions of the identities of the parties involved and the nature of their conflict at the same time that parallel struggles for dominance went on within them. Some contending groups find it in their interests to portray the combatants and the struggle between them as ethnic, while others deny such claims and advance others (Assal, & Abdul-Jalil, 2015, pp. 218).[18]

In the midst of what was termed as "senseless conflict", people killed in the chaotic political and military race were found with eyes gauged out, their heads nailed, bodies multilated, and animals axed. The reported that came out of South Sudan during the period of 2013 through 2018 will be a shameful reading that no one would be happy to read. The scores of

---

18   Assal, Munzoul A. M. & Abdul-Jalil, Musa Adam. (2015). Past, present, and future. FIFTY YEARS OF ANTHROPOLOGY IN SUDAN. *Chr. Michelsen Institute.* https://www.cmi.no/publications/file/5499-past-present-and-future.pdf

people killed, displaced, villaged burned and the swapping of cattle from across the country is unimaginable. This is why war is defined as the scourge of civilization. It destroys prosperity and kills an enormous number of people—combatants and civilians both are swept into its maw (Schake, 2017).[19] The judgement is to the living, and for them to take serious notes of all that has taken place in South Sudan.

Governance

Since Sudan's independence in 1956, governments and rebel forces have continued to govern through the chiefs' courts. In 1983, mutinied Sudan Armed Forces formed the Sudan People's Liberation Army (SPLA). The SPLA's rapid success meant that it found itself governing vast areas of rural South Sudan and, therefore, had a government-like relationship to those it governed. In the early years of the SPLA, Marxist thinking prompted them to question the legitimacy of the chiefs' courts because of their association with colonial rule.[20]

---

19   Schake, K. (2017). What Causes War? *Orbis, 61(4), 449–462.* https://doi-org.lopes.idm.oclc.org/10.1016/j.orbis.2017.08.002. https://lopes.idm.oclc.org/login?url=https://search.ebscohost.com/login.aspx?direct=true&db=edselp&AN=S0030438717300698&site=eds-live&scope=site&custid=s8333196&groupid=main&profile=eds1

20   Pendle, N. R. (2020). Politics, prophets, and armed mobilizations: competition and continuity over registers of authority in South Sudan's conflicts. *JOURNAL OF EASTERN AFRICAN STUDIES, 14(1),* 43–62. https://doi-org.lopes.idm.oclc.org/10.1080/17531055.2019.1708545. https://lopes.idm.oclc.org/login?url=https://search.ebscohost.com/login.aspx?direct=true&db=edswss&AN=000506324700001&site=eds-live&scope=site&custid=s8333196&groupid=main&profile=eds1

Before the Europeans arrived in Africa, Africans have their unique social and political structures. The government as it known today is so foreign to Africans so is democracy. The tribes in South Sudan, and Sudan at large lived independently more like nation-states. They were able to choose their leaders and arrange leadership successions with minimal crisis. At the same time, they had legal mechanisms where they resolve disputes among themselves. The tribal courts used to deliver equitable decisions, which safeguarded physical security as well as material wealth security. The govenance in the lenses of African traditions and the modern time converged at the power station.

South Sudan is blessed with energtic academics who want to give back to their country. The country was started from the scratch, yet people are willing to start where the world is, not going to where the started some centuries ago. Even with all that, the Government has not been easy on the think tanks whose desire is to make South Sudan catch up with rests of the world. "I am convinced with a shred of doubt that South Sudan has become another sad scene in the long episode of dictatorship in Africa and I am determined to oppose this dictatorship and authoritarianism with everything I have got," (Awolich, 2021).[21] This is not the first time that people who have dictated that their times and talents poked the Government in the face.

In more than a dozen times, patriots have been forced out

21   Awolich, Abraham. (November 25, 2021). Top official from leading think tank in S. Sudan resigns. *Sudan Tribune.* https://sudantribune.com/article226415/?fbclid=IwAR0G72yYjw12IdMX2asOZiK7jkdB-WhTkdreXn1wKAKL5m6vVT7IlpQlVNXo

of the country because they did not support the agendas of the regime of the day. Since South Sudan attained its independence, quite a number of South Sudanese intellectuals relocated to South Sudan for nation-building and reconstruction of the country. "Reference to your letter dated the 2nd of August 2021, asking me to tender in my resignation from the Sudd Institute, and in line with the mission of the Sudd Institute, this note serves as my resignation both from the position of managing director and from the Sudd Institute entirely," said Abraham Awolich.[22] The resignation was tendered while in the United States. It took coordinated efforts to get members of the People's Coalition of Civil Action (PCCA) out of South Sudan in the height of negative wobblings.

Leadership in Indigenous African Societies

Long before the colonial powers and Arab religious crusades, Africans have their unique leadership structures. Among the Dinkas of South Sudan, leaders have both the divine powers as well as the social skills to be able to rule amicably. It is believed that are leaders can solve social and political crises. And at the same time intervene natural disasters that were often believed to be divine in nature. The nature of things are in South Sudan has not made it possible for much transition to be realized. Across

---

22   Awolich, Abraham. (November 25, 2021). Top official from leading think tank in S. Sudan resigns. *Sudan Tribune*. https://sudantribune. com/article226415/?fbclid=IwAR0G72yYjw12IdMX2asOZiK7jkdB-WhTkdreXn1wKAKL5m6vVT7IlpQlVNXo

South Sudan, East Africa and the world, religion including spirit possession is playing a role in armed mobilizations. Many international actors who engage in these conflicts to bring peace or reshape the war carry with them assumptions of a division between religion and politics (Pendle, 2020).[23] There is much more to be done.

The State of South Sudan is yet to adopt lots of the modern day things. Many South Sudanese still believe in traditional divine powers. In many instances, people extend a call to God in times of uncertainties. Not once, but many times that the ruling elites goes to their roots to seek advices as to how to clingue to power and push their opponents to the edges. The spearmasters have been kept close to the thrones despite spiritual leaders having little or no knowledge the political ideologies and power thirsts. The memories of the past are as fresh as people can recall.

In Dinka political theory and practice people's experience of the divinely derived abilities of certain lineages leads to those lineages becoming the focus of communities of people with lesser religious powers (for everyone has some) who has established themselves around them. People experience the practical

23   Pendle, N. R. (2020). Politics, prophets, and armed mobilizations: competition and continuity over registers of authority in South Sudan's conflicts. *JOURNAL OF EASTERN AFRICAN STUDIES, 14(1)*, 43–62. https://doi-org.lopes.idm.oclc.org/10.1080/17531055.2019.170 8545. https://lopes.idm.oclc.org/login?url=https://search.ebscohost.com/login.aspx?direct=true&db=edswss&AN=000506324700001&site=eds-live&scope=site&custid=s8333196&groupid=main&profile=eds1

day-to-day religious abilities of a lineage through the efficacy of particular individuals. Communities are created by people seeking to associate themselves with these individuals. In a sense, a religiously powerful individual enables the formation of a community. This is recognized in social practice and religious imagery, where the person of a powerful master of the fishing spear often represents the community as a whole.[24]

Power

In the South Sudanese society, long before the introduction of centralized governance, South Sudanese have two major form of government: monarchy and chiefdoms. The power through monarchy was passed do via King's lineage, and their was not much say community who would over the highest throne. In the case chiefdoms, quite a number of factors play roles at who take over the leadership. There often power struggle, those whose aspired to leader do certain things to show themselves that they can leader in all certain. All this summed up tribes, govenance and power in the case of South Sudan.

Like all societies undergoing rapid transition, the resumption of war brought a cleavage over the many pressing social, cultural, political and economic issues between military and the

24   Mawson, A. N. M. (1991). "Bringing What People Want": Shrine Politics among the Agar Dinka. *Africa (Edinburgh University Press)*, 61(3), 354–369. https://doi-org.lopes.idm.oclc.org/10.2307/1160030. https://lopes.idm.oclc.org/login?url=https://search.ebscohost.com/login.aspx?direct=true&db=rlh&AN=11675250&site=eds-live&scope=site

civilians population.[25]

At the dawn of South Sudan's independence, South Sudanese went through excruciating experiences; South Sudan's political leaders banged against the thin line. There was no time and enrgey put rominent politicians kepts the wounds of liberation struggle close to flame, and got easily exposed to the tribal rifes. In the name of national cohesion, President Salva Kiir and vice president Dr. Riek Machar swerved into prohibited political territories. When Government's institutions, heads of the departments, agents and all the partners linked to the government of the day have been consistently wrong, the issue of bad governance become no longer debatable. The South Sudanese society is very complex, broad from the top, and narrow at the bottom. And for South Sudanese have little knowledge of what Government is all about, they have lived in grey area of the social and political strucures for centuries, and under numerous Governments that viewed the rural people as not their own. With the 1899 Anglo-Egypt treaty Britain grafted itself onto Egypt's old Empire.

Within the time past, and at the course of half a century, Southern Sudanese experienced the changing face of that empire, initially more Egyptian than Anglo, and more Southern Sudanese than Egyptian (Johnson, 2016, pp.100). Since the time of Ali Dynasty (Turkiyah) 1821–1885, Mahdiyah: 1885–1899, and Anglo-Egyptian rule: 1899–1956, the lower part of

25   Jok, Madut Jok. Sudan: Race, Religion, And Violence. *Oneworld Publications.* Oxford, 2007

the Great Nile was neglected, looked upon as a place for food production, a place of natural beauty, and where twilight spectacularly glows the sky. The British initial appearance in the Sudan has left behind staints of the things were not Sudan. The British's scrambling for control of the Sudan and its people is a very unique legacy of "divide and rule."

The decision of the British government to occupy the Sudan in the last decade of the nineteenth century resulted in part from the British fear that the other colonial powers (Italy, France, and Belgium) might take advantage of the Sudan's instability to acquire territories previously annexed to Egypt. Apart from these considerations, Britain wanted to establish control over the Nile and safeguard its economic interests in Egypt (Abushouk, 2010).[26]

The Anglo-Egyptian Treaty of 1899 ushered in a period of joint Anglo-Egyptian rule. While the British did make permanent and lasting contributions to the creation of a modern Sudan during this time, most, if not all of its development projects were focused on the Nile River valley (Carolan, 2021). The indigenious people of the Sudan were not treated humanely, no services or programs to improve lives of the millions along the major rivers, and in the rural Sudan. As a result of leaving the region in hung of politicio-religious nightmares, Sudan had

---

26   Abushouk, Ahmed Ibrahim. (2010). The Anglo-Egyptian Sudan: From Collaboration Mechanism to Party Politics, 1898–1956. *The Journal of Imperial and Commonwealth History*. Vol. 38, No. 2, June 2010, pp. 207–236. https://www.academia.edu/3723516/

been at war with itself since independence from Britain in 1956. Some localized conflicts in the old Sudan fitted tribes against themselves while the successive Governments in Khartoum did nothing improve relationships among citizens. There has an enormous human's loss in the Sudan through fierce infighting.

The heaviest toll on the South Sudanese took place during the second Sudanese war, when population dispersal took on a range of forms, broadly represented in this article through a discourse of refugees and self-settled refugees. Such classifications distinguish pre-migration, flight, and post-migration experiences, as well as attendant rights, struggles and opportunities.[27]

Vision and Governance

Every liberation movement is triggered by injustice and vision to restore lost dignity. The Sudan and South Sudanese conflict is no exception. Since the inception of Sudan's independence, there have been many military and political unrests. The British Administration took Sudanese as they were culturally and religiously. The British Administration administered Sudanese as northerners and Southerners. In the Southern regions, independence in a united inherited from the Condominium seemed impossible. The North and South had evolved along completely

27   Impey, A. (2013). Keeping in touch via cassette: tracing Dinka songs from cattle camp to transnational audio-letter. *Journal of African Cultural Studies, 25(2), 197–210.* https://lopes.idm.oclc.org/login?url=https://search.ebscohost.com/login.aspx?direct=true&db=edb&AN=87820879&site=eds-live&scope=site

different lines. The spirit of division created by the Southern Policy led to the sense of hostility which erupted into civil war even before independence was officially declared (Dani, 2012. Pp. 240).[28] When the British left the Sudan, Sudanese in the South had raised a number of contentious issues, starting with the 1947 Juba Round Table, followed by the Torit Uprising of August 18, 1955, and the subsequent Anya-Nya Movement that lasted for 17 years. All those wranglings took the space in the history because there were individuals who had put forth their visions for the Sudanese at large.

John Garang's vision of a New Sudan that respects the rights of all its peoples is attractive to the politically sophisticated class in these borderlands. Under Yusif Kuwa, the late SPLM/A leader in the Nuba Mountains, a concerted effort was made to promote it by encouraging local culture and developing local government (Young, 2003).[29]

The governance of the indigenous Africans had always been regarded by European colonial powers as hectic of a job, yet the invading powers want ed the Africans conquered, and their natural resources seized. The exploitation started from onset;

---

28   Dani, Fatiha. (2012). The Growth Nationalism in Sudan under Anglo-Egypt Rule (1899-1956). A Doctoral Thesis for African Civilization. *University of Oran*. https://theses.univ-oran1.dz/document/42201234t.pdf

29   Young, J. (2003). Sudan: Liberation Movements, Regional Armies, Ethnic Militias & Peace. *Review of African Political Economy, 30(97)*, *423–434*.   https://lopes.idm.oclc.org/login?url=https://search.ebscohost.com/login.aspx?direct=true&db=edb&AN=11936325&site=eds-live&-scope=site&custid=s8333196&groupid=main&profile=eds1

human were sent into slavery for free labor in the new world, their freedom taken away, both in the contintnetla of Africa as well as places where they were being enslaved. The Arabs in sub-sahara Africa, particularly in the Sudan acted as the middlemen between the Arabs in the middle East and the white settlers who were their just for colonialization and chritinization of indigenious Africans.

On the land, the Arabs settlers had grand agenda; make Nile Valley their home forever, transformed cultures, assimilated natives by means of religion, and defined people's relationships. Such protracted neglect was responsible for the revolt witnessed in Southern Sudan's town of Torit on August 18, 1955 and beyond. In a conventinonal society, all members must be treated equally regardless of their ethnic, tribal or religious backgrounds. The policies of the Sudanese Government on Southern Sudanese clearly showed disparaity. At some points, the Sudanese Government negotiated the digging of Jonglei canal without full consensus Southern tribes that lived along the Sudd. The project then became part and parcel of the Sudanese second civil war.

The Dinka, Shilluk, and Nuer who were directly affected feared the drastic changes the canal would bring to their way of life. They would not accept the prospect of life without the migration to the toich during the dry season, when they would find fish and improve the milk yield of their cows. They also teared the prospect of alien people being settled in their midst,

and the possibility of conflict (Suliman, 1997, p. 115-116).[30]

The unity of purpose shown by South Sudanese when they fought colonial power, and during the many years of war of liberation is a living evidence that South Sudanese willone day live in peaceful and prosperous country. There are prerequisites when it comes to running a country and making livable. The actors from all levels of the South Sudanese society just need to rise above ethnocentric, and take the whole as truly their.

We Must Accommodate all the Tribes

South Sudan has 64 legally recognized tribes, all of which have their traditional social and political systems. The tribes, especially those that make their living from farming have evolved greatly, and have adopted some modern styles of leadership. There is supposedly a lesson learned from the old Sudan; and that is making sure that all citizens feels at home. The first civil war was a result of long-term economic of Turko–Egyptian rule, the southern Sudanese had developed a strong African identity. Economic dominance by the northerners, along with subjugation by foreign traders and slavers, led to a general consensus that they were different. Consequently, the 'south' emerged as a political concept in opposition to the 'north', which was predominantly identified with Islam and an Arab culture

---

30   Suliman, Mohamed (1997). Civil War in Sudan: The Impact of Ecological Degradation, Contributions in Black Studies. *A Journal of African and Afro-American Studies, Vol. 15 (7).* https://scholarworks.umass.edu/cibs/vol15/iss1/7

(Raftopoulos, & Alexander, 2006, p.10-11).[31] For any country to remain united, no part of the country or tribes should feel left out of the national cake. People have to receive their fair share if there is such a thing called entitlement or they should reaps what they have sown. The politics of inclusion is not necessarily related to forming government; it has also a lot to do with crafting nationhood (Morris, 2011).[32]

Back to the core of what make societies great, people in position of power have to do more, and exceed citizens' expectations. In that regards, leaders need to be observant, taking everything seriously and discharging their duties accordingly. As to citizens' physical security; the traditional setting have evolved; there is hydrid systems, local police, local courts, and shopping centers that supports the local communities. The governance in the farming communites has been modernized. On the others hands, cattle rearing communities continue to follow their traditional way of life; they seasonally move from place to place in search of water and pastures. While the nation is moving toward modern States, there are challenges throughout the country as many cultures collide, tribes in the South Sudan have been trying to forge one national identity.

---

31   Raftopoulos, Brian, & Alexander, Karin. (2006). Peace in the Balance: The Crisis in Sudan. *Journal of Eastern African Studies. Institute for Justice and Reconciliation.* http://africanminds.co.za/wp-content/uploads/2012/05/Peace%20in%20the%20Balance%20-%20The%20Crisis%20in%20Sudan.pdf

32   Morris, Nsamba Adam. (2011). State Building and Development in South Sudan. *African Research and Resource Forum.* https://www.academia.edu/26585030/State_Building_and_Development_in_South_Sudan

The past is always a perfect guide. The works of colonial powers and that of the northerns Sudanese who controlled every aspect of the Sudan is a serious note that should be revisited if South Sudan is to made great. It is imperative that whatever went wrong in the past ought not be repeated. There is a great deal of literature on how Sudan was governed, and how Southern Sudan was isolated from north Sudan. The socio-political structure introduced and left behind by the Anglo–condominium rule created social and regional inequality. Along the Nile River area, education facilities improved, and the infrastructure and economy were developed while the rest of the country remained underdeveloped and neglected (Raftopoulos, & Alexander, 2006, p.9).[33] It is from all these sociopolitical malpractices that South Sudan need to design their own destiny.

Moving forward, history has it that no nation in the world can succeed without taking care of it diverse civil population. It is not new that some minorities would feel annihilated, but the gap between the powerful and the wealth should be narrowed to allow for easy stirring. The north–south dichotomy was shaped not only by the legacy of colonial rule but also by the inconsistent policies of the independence movement (Raftopoulos, & Alexander, 2006, p.10). Point to note, multi-ethnic States require far more interwoven social fabrics or tribes

---

33   Raftopoulos, Brian, & Alexander, Karin. (2006). Peace in the Balance: The Crisis in Sudan. *Journal of Eastern African Studies. Institute for Justice and Reconciliation.* http://africanminds.co.za/wp-content/uploads/2012/05/Peace%20in%20the%20Balance%20-%20The%20Crisis%20in%20Sudan.pdf

not close to the power would distablize the country leading to sericous long-term failures. In many instances, there is incompability across the board as many tribs feel annihilated by the major tribes. The politicians from all walks of life tend to take shortcuts in politics. While many have the will to serve the civil population, they often exploit the commons to get their way around. There is no doubt, majority of South Sudanese are not politically informed. When the South Sudan was preparing for a measure referendum, the Sudanese general election that was scheduled to take place for the Southern region, Abyei, Nuba Mountain and Southern Blue were due for referendum and popular vote, some political aspirants took to the bush when they lost election, and all claimed election's rigging.

Once in a while, new political maneuvering involved high profile warlords such as George Athor Deng (Dinka tribe), Peter Gatdet Yak (Nuer tribe), and junior officers such as Johnson Olony and Robert Gwang (Shilluk tribe), David Yau Yau from the Murle tribe, and Peter Lorot from the Didinga tribe. The tendencies of a failing state are more ominous than the auguries of state fragility. State failure is fundamentally a source of preventable full-blown crisis on the international arena (Okeke, Idike, Akwara, Okorie, & Ibiam, 2021).

The arm race torched down some villages, drove civilians away from their homes as the regional army(the SPLA) battle the renegades, and autonomous government presided over by the Giant warlords (pres. Salva Kiir & his vice, Dr. Riek Machar) were tested. The mass displacement of civil population across South Sudan was deeply rooted in geopolitical trajectories of the current state of affairs in Africa as well as in the Middle East. The charges also goes to the policies of the affluent nations of the world whose economics interests help in tearing apart nations of the developing world. The problems of the developing nations are so interconnected and attributed to the inability to be economically vibrant despite the abundant of material and human resources at their disposal.

The Troika and the CPA-2005

After 21-years of bloodiest civil war, Sudanese finally arrived at what became known as the Comprehensive Peace Agreement in 2005. The peace was broken by African states and midwived by the United States, the United Kingdoms and the Kingdoms of Norway (the Troka). The CPA's implementation raised some concerns because Sudan's previous civil wars proved that conflicts in Sudan do not stay there. There interconnectedness of wars of identities to the rests of the world gave observors reasons to make some recommendations as to what should be done and what should not be done. Okech Alfred (2007) wrote that, "the civil wars in the Sudan have transcended national borders and become regional wars" (Alfred, 2007, p. 27). Any return to war between the North and South will also have regional components. Since the signing of the CPA in 2005, the international engagement has supported such a concentration of forces significantly – politically, economically, at the level of development cooperation and also at the level of military training for the SPLA in order to become the South Sudanese national army (Pospisil, 2014, p. 9).[34] It remains to be seen whether the supports rendered by those who wants to see South Sudan as a stable country has yielded any fruits.

Throughout the world, the United States of America and her Allies plays crucial roles in keeping the world's peace. As the most the powerful and the richest nation in the world, the US have international outreaches that oversees political crises, and funds efforts to restore peace whereas there is a conflict. During the many years of civil war in the Sudan, the United States, and other western powers; Russia and Great Britain have switched sides, not once, but many times. There were in-stances where the Government of the Untied States, especially during the Reagan's Era supported the Sudanese Government in Kharotum. It was pretty much about the Oil that was discov-ered by American Oil Giant Chevron in 1978. The discovery of oil in the Sudan played in the hands of elites in the Sudan as well as in the Middle East, the region of the world that shared a lot with the Sudanese.

As the world's largest economy, and the most technological-ly advanced nation, with vast military presence in the world, the United States is always on the lookout, scanning the world for possible investments as well as checking around for possible threat to their against their global dominance. With all that, the

---

34   Pospisil, J. (2014). Civil War in South Sudan: Bloody Ethno-Poli-tics and a Failed International Engagement. (PolicyPaper / Österreichisches Institut für Internationale Politik, 3). Wien: Österreichisches *Institut für Internationale Politik (oiip)*. https://nbn-resolving.org/urn:nbn:de:0168-ssoar-58638-1

United States has a defined interest that shape the world in one way or the other. And for the Sudanese, just like other developing nations of the world, it often takes an external force for an internal conflict to be resolved. The Sudanese people have been fighting themselves fro more thant 5 decades, but peace was permanently reached with the brokering of African States, United States, Kingdoms of Norway and the United Kingdoms.

"The Sudan Peace Act was passed by Congress, signed into law by President, and Senator John Danforth was named Special Envoy to Sudan in a ceremony in the White House Rose Garden on September 6, 2001. The administration got behind this endeavor, and their efforts led to an agreement."[35]

This is to give credit that no war in the developing world come to an end without the involvement of the nations like the United States of America. In all the Sudan's 21-years civil war, US had been involved in Sudan's affairs in one way or another. The US administration shifted gears in all the years Sudan had been at war with Southern based armed guerrilla Movement. The last switch was for the better, the Khartoum based regime resolved to ending the two-decades war.

The United States, pushed by domestic interest groups such as evangelical Christians and the Congressional Black Caucus, expressed outspoken unhappiness over Khartoum's handling of the war with the SPLM/A, the human-rights situation, including alleged government support for slavery, and its welcoming

---

35   Sam Brownback. (2007). A Remarkable Journey of Faith and Compassion: From Power to Power. *Thomas Nelson*

environment toward international terrorist groups. Washington put Sudan on its list of state supporters of terrorism in 1993, an action that resulted in additional U.S. sanctions against Sudan (Berry, 2015, pp. 292-3).[36]

The efforts by the United States, Kingdoms of Norway and the United Kingdoms led to successful vote for independence. The referendum conducted in 2011 was a very closed exercise of Self-Determination granted in the first phase of the peace negotistion. The South Sudanese officially split from rest of the Sudan, formed their own nation, and subsequently joined the East Africa community after the approval of their application to be part of the Swahili speaking nations. All along, and during the war of liberation, nation of the Great Lake supported Sudan People's Liberation Movement/Army in so many ways; including harboring the rebels and giving them places to train their fighters, helping in logistics. This is not to forget the proxy wars fiught in the South Sudanese soil by interest group. For example, the Sudanese Government trained and supplied Uganda's rebels, the Lord's Resistance Army (LRA) with weaponries, and logistical supports to wage war against the Uganda's Government.

In one way or the other, the Sudanese conflict was a very complicated war. The Africans and the Arabs in the Middle East were pretty involved, idealogically and materially supports to warring parties on both sides of the conflict. With the helps of

---

36   Berry, L. B. (2015). Sudan, a country study / Federal Research Division, Library of Congress; edited by LaVerle Berry. *Fifth edition.* https://permanent.fdlp.gov/gpo63176/CS_Sudan.pdf#

African States in the Great Lake, the Sudan People's Liberation Movement/Army stood against all odds, keeping up with Sudanese army that had huge supports from Islamists in North Africa as well as Middle East nation that envisioned Sudan as the brideges between the Arabs States and the African States in the South of the Africa as a continent. The political landscape in much of Africa is tribal based, tribes play crucial roles in social and political developments of the countries.

Not All States Are Created Equal

In the dawn of Southern Sudanese preparing for the historic Referendum, there were legitimate concerns raised by experienced scholars, civil society organizations, religious leaders and regional research institutions. The Sudanese governance problem was deeply rooted in the way successive Governments in Kharotum were setup. From the day one, there were unequal political representation, and that credited to be major cause of social and political unrests in the country. In a multicultural, multilingual, and multireligious nation like the Sudan, leaders ought to do more than just seeking peace with no social and political programs for the people in the country. "Peace is more than the absence of war. Once the last gun shot is fired, there is still an enormous amount of work to be done. As citizens of the world, we need to come together and offer support to communities ravaged by war."[37] This is exactly what was need in the Republic of Sudan before Southern Sudan's referendum could take place.

As far as the facts of the long conflict are concern, the Sudanese on both sides of the political divide were not prepared for the outcome of the historic referendum, and that had been evidenced by the continued fighting in South Sudan and in the Sudan despite country having been divided up into two, majority muslims in the north and majority Sudanese in the south because on the religious and cultural values. The conflict in the old Sudan became history of the past, but the problem of governance in both countries had not addressed, and that unresolved fundamental problem haunted both Sudanses and South Sudanese after the split. The fight for independent South Sudan had not been without obstacles. Ever since, some South Sudanese have mistakenly put-up with the successive Khartoum-based regimes for reasons known to them. In the South, it was squarely Southern Sudanese against South Sudanese. The Khartoum had been very effective in using "divide and rule" strategy.

The most significant military organization outside SPLA control in the late 1990s was a faction of the South Sudan United Democratic Alliance (SSUDA) and dissident elements of the South Sudan Defense Force (SSDF). The SSDF was the military wing of the SSUDA. Created in 1997, the organization became an umbrella group that once brought together a variety

37   Jenkins, Diana (2014). Huff Post. Peace Is More Than the Absence of War. *Huff Post.* https://www.huffpost.com/entry/the-absence-of-war_b_5176243

of Southern militias and political groups, all of which were subject to regular defections and factional battles. The Equatoria Defense Force (EDF), which operated in the area around Juba and Torit, was perhaps the most politically effective group in the SSDF. Most of its fighters were Latuku and Lokoya. It was generally believed that Khartoum supported the EDF. The EDF signed a merger agreement with the SPLM/A in March 2004, although it was not clear how many EDF fighters accepted it. The Bor Group consisted primarily of SPLA defectors from South Bor. The governor of East Equatoria charged in 2006 that remnants of the EDF continued to carry out attacks and be a threat to security because they received arms from Khartoum (Berry, 2015, pp. 266).[38]

For any new way forward, the cores causes of war to the Sudanese conflicts were to be addressed as a preparation for the new beginning. Whether South Sudanese remain part of the united Sudan or have their separate country, there were certain things that had to be put in place in order for common citizens to live in harmony and collectively embark on the nation-building and the State building. The two Sudans became hubs of violence conflicts after the independence, the social and political differences that torn apart the country muted, and each country was faced with new problem. The world, through international organizations and intergovernmental organizations tried their

---

38   Berry, L. B. (2015). Sudan, a country study / Federal Research Division, Library of Congress; edited by LaVerle Berry. Fifth edition. https://permanent. fdlp.gov/gpo63176/CS_Sudan.pdf#

level best shape the future of the two Republics. Unfortunately, every advice fell on a deaf ears.

The situations in the two Sudans remain volatile, and unforgiving. Since the signing of the CPA-2005 between the Government of Sudan and the SPLM, many oppressed Sudanese in the north grew bolder and started to wage their own liberation again the Sudanese Government. The highly anticipated separation of South from rests of the Sudan motivated political dissidents to seek avenue for equitable distribution power sharing and fair sharing of national resources.

It is obvious, therefore, that the secession of the South would not necessarily end conflicts in Sudan without resolving the national identity crisis in the North and establishing an equitable governance system in the South. Likewise, the prospects for unity of the country do not necessarily cease wit the independence of the South.[39]

---

39   Deng, Francis Mading, forwarded by Kevin M. Cahill, Sudan at the Brink. Fordham University Press and the Institute for International Humanitarian Affairs, New York, 2010.

CHAPTER TWO

Tribes in South Sudan

The flash point came at Bor 16 May 1983, when the ex-Anyan-ya soldiers in Battalion 105 refused orders to be transferred to the north. After the repulsed an attack by the Sudanese army, it met up with Anyanya 2 in the bush by pre-arrangement and headed for Ethiopia (Johnson, 2016, pp. 141).

Tribes in South Sudan formed the basis for social, political and economic aspects of the nation, and they also defines power as utilized across the relationships spectrum. The Republic of South Sudan comprised of 64 tribes with possibly ethnicities in hundreds if not thousands. It took British a while to get to all the villages in the rural tribal nations, and it was not

Taken from Paanluelwel.com - The map showed Jieng's tribes in Jonglei state: Hol Dinka, Nyarweng Dinka, Bor Dinka, and Twic East Dinka.

for the missionaries to for learn about unique cultures in the hidden forests of Southern Sudan. The Chrisitians Missions set up in Southern Sudan in the early 1900s cleared way for South Sudanese to see outside world, and for them to learn foreign langauges.

The earlier settlers in the Sudan, Turks and Arabs did very little to change people in the villages or sent kids to schools. Throughout most of South Sudan transition to Christianity, Missions were the places of worhsips as well as places of studies. For example, the West Nile Jieng refers to church schools as Paan-Abun, meaning clergy's place. Education took sometimes before it become something people desired to do for the betterment of themselves as well as for their country as a whole. In the Upper Nile, Jieng referred to them as Hon e Gaar (studies House).

In an effort to curb Dinka domination and strengthen personal access to political power, Joseph Lagu, a Madi from Equatoria, began to agitate for the re-division of the South into three regions. He rallied support among non-Dinkas, emphasizing subgroup rivalries and cultivating fears with respect to Dinka dominance under the provisions of the Addis Ababa Agreement. As he was not able to prevail over his subgroup rivals politically, he allied with Sudan's president Nimeiri, who seized the opportunity to foment divisions among the South Sudanese. Nimeiri dissolved the regional government structures by presidential decree and established three regions, all of which were to be led by Joseph Lagu's Allies. The decree violated the Addis Ababa Agreement and was one of the triggers for the resumption of civil war with the North a few months later.[40]

The earlier white explorers who visited Sudan in the 1900 documented a detailed accounts of the relationships among the various tribes in the Sudan, particularly the cattle rearing communities in what was Southern Sudan. Everything has always centered around tribal affiliations, and traditional political was skewedlyd defined by how much a leader dealt with outsiders, particularly members of other tribes. In the olden days, South Sudan's tribes have power that was either in the hand of a tribal chief, a spiritual leader, a spreadmaster or a King. All of those leaders possessed some kinds of powers that given ultimate power over affairs of their society as each tribal territory was ruled much more like a country. In the Dinkalands and the Nuerlands, supreme leaders were chiefs with unlimted powers, and sometime organized fights that involved raiding into neighboring tribes's territories. One of the first Social Anthropologist to live among South Sudanese tribes has the following account:

All the important prophets about whom we have information gained their prestige by directing successful raids on the Dinka, for these raids were carried out in the names of the spirits which promised rich booty by their lips. No extensive raids were undertaken without the permission and guidance of prophets, who received instructions from the sky-gods in

40   De Juan, A. (2013). Devolving Ethnic Conflicts: The Role of Subgroup Identities for Institutional Intergroup Settlements. *Civil Wars*, *15(1), 78*. doi:10.1080/13698249.2013.781304. https://lopes.idm.oclc.org/login?url=http://search.ebscohost.com/login.aspx?direct=true&db=edb&AN=87373928&site=eds-live&scope=site

dreams and trances about time and objective of the attack, and often they accompanied them in person performed sacrifices before battle.[41]

British in Southern Sudan in the Early 1900s

In the early days of the British Administration in the then Southern Sudan, the African tribes in the South did not have centralized governments or system of governance. It is also important to note that before the occupation of Egypt, Britain had no direct political or commercial dealings in the Sudan. In the 18th century, the British people and Government had no specific knowledge of that country which was to them just a part 'darkest Africa.'[42] The tribes considred themselves as country in sense that a chief in a certain clan or groups of clans ruled more like heads of States. When the British arrived, there was a need for the tribes to be introduced to the central government as a new form of administering the many tribes and clans. The introduction was not an easy thing, especially in the nilotics groups such as the Dinka/Jiengs and the Nuers.

"At the arrival of the British there were in existence two areas of acute political conflict immediately north and south of Nuerland. In the South, the Nuer were steadily expanding at the

---

41   Evans-Pritchard, E.E. The Nuer: A description of the Modes of Livelihood and Political Institutions of a Nilotic People. Oxford University Presss, 1940.
42   Dani, Fatiha. (2012). The Growth Nationalism in Sudan under Anglo-Egypt Rule (1899-1956). A Doctoral Thesis for African Civilization. University of Oran. https://theses.univ-oran1.dz/document/42201234t.pdf

expense of the Southern Dinka. In March 1905 the Inspector of Upper Nile, H. H. Wilson; reported that the Ghol Dinka were "in a horrible state of fear of the Nuers" and that they wished to migrate, en masse to Khor Fullus at the mouth of the Sobat river. The condition of their neighbors, the Nyareweng Dinka was even worse; Wilson found them living in the forest, "like game" for fear of the Nuers and remarked that they were "only one example of them, any (Dinka tribes) who through the absence of any security are deteriorating; into wild men of the woods." The request of the Ghol to migrate to the north was turned down because the Khor Fullus itself was another region of acute friction. Dinka refugees from Nuer control had moved into this relatively accessible region at about the time of the ar- rival of the British and, like the small peoples of Western Bahr al-Ghazal; they had promptly offered to pay tribute and place themselves under Government protection. Thinking themselves thus, secure "they kept up a kind of guerrilla warfare against the Nuer." From their protected base or sanctuary they launched hit-and-run raids and rustled Nuer cattle. Wilson also reported that these Dinka, refugees- missed no opportunity to vilify the Nuers to the Government." (Badal, 1977, p. 49).43

The word governance in the minds of many South Sudanese does look exactly the same; some regard it as eutopia, an ab- stract foreign term that does not necessary means much to the political functions in the country. For much of the self-rule,

---

43   Badal, Raphael Koba. (1977). British Administration in Souther Sudan, 1900-1956: A Study in Colonial Neglect. ProQuest LLC. https://eprints.soas. ac.uk/29707/1/10752679.pdf

not all communities have sent competent Representatives to the Regional governments. There have been instances where those who took up people's seats went on to enrich themselves while others strictly conformed to the interests of their peope they represented. A good example is the case where some people opposed government led by their own son, and instead chose to oppose the policies based on what they saw a a disservice to the governed. In 1974, some members of the Dinka enthnic Group were opposed Abel Alier's governmental, particularly the endorsement of the Jonglei Canal project, and as forwarded by the Sudanese Government in Khartoum.

Ovewhelmed by returning refugees and the recnstruction of, the regional government in Juba had no time and vehicles to consult with the chiefs or their people before signing of the agreement in June 1974. The europhoria of autonomy could not hide a history of distrust and seventeen years of civil war, all of which aroused deep suspicions in the Southerners. Joshua Dau Diu from Fanjak in the Sudd was the first to curse the canal in the assembly at Juba.[44] Page 202, para. 3

For some individuals who want to create a tribal and a monolithic society where citizens only follow tribal alignment, their goal is have rivalry among different tribes and clans within the country. A multicultural, multiethnic, and multireligious country like South Sudanese, people's representatives should pick and choose political stances that serve interests of the people they represent, and leading in the Executive branch ought to

---

44   Collins, Roberts O. The Nile. Yale University Press/New Haven& London, 2002.

expand their leadership vision to the point where some of their deeds would reflect on their legacies. It's from such premise that the people of South Sudan would have a place they call country, and the politics that often divide citizens along tribal lines will cease to exist.

Looking back to the past regional administration, Jiengs in the governments have been the ones who held themselves to the highest standards with some taking interests of the people they represented so seriously. As noted by Robert Collins, the notable opposition to Abel Alier's regional government were the Dinkas/Jiengs. The areas chosen were allegedly going to be turned into farmland by the Jonglei Project, millions to be displaced and thousands from Egyptian to tend the land for agricultural functions.

The Regional government does not wish and will not associate itself with politics that tend to maintain and perpetuate status quo in the Region...We are [not] to remain as a sort of human zoo for anthrologists, tourists, environmentalists and adventurers from developed countries of Europe to study us, our orgins, our plights, the size of our skulls and the shape and length customary scars on our forehead. I wish to say that although this [Jonglei] is a Central Government project, the regional Government supports it and stands for it. If we have to drive our people to paradise with sticks, we will do it for their own good and the good of those who come after us.[45] Robert O. Collins. Page 204, para. 3.

---

45   Collins, Roberts O. The Nile. Yale University Press/New Haven& London, 2002.

From the getgo, it was crytal clear that there were people who were pretty much opposed to the project in its entirety. Given the complexity of the project, it was later discovered that those who were opposed to the project were acting on the best interest of the general population; much of the lives around and near Nile basin is dependence on abundance waters of the Nile River as source of life for many in the region. The perennial overflow should not be seen as so threathening the lives of the locals. Some developmental projects along the Nile could have been strategied not the giant project that would drain the Sudd, making commute to the water source so cumbersome to the locals. Three decades later, those who were opposed the Jonglei Project remains vocal and wary about the revival of the canal. There are many fears when it comes to draining of the Sudd.

Before the opponents of Jonglei took to the streets of Juba, the opposition to the canal had been expressed in the Southern regional assembly by Joshua Dau Diu from Fangak and the late Benjamin Bol Akok, the representative from Aweil and the deputy speaker of the assembly, supported by Clement Mboro, Oliver Albino, Stephen Lam, and Simon Morris. They were motivated solely by their dislike of Jonglei. In fact, they intended to use the agreement to build the canal as a means to unseat the government of Abel Alier, and towards that end they rallied the students from Juba Commercial Secondary school to protest against the canal.[46]

---

46   Collins, Roberts O. The Waters of the Nile: Hydropolitics and the Jonglei Canal, 1900-1988. *Markus Wiener Publishers/Princeton, 1996.*

State Power in South Sudan

State power in South Sudan is at the mercy of the most revered warlords. The nation of South Sudan was founded by both ballots and bullets. South Sudanese fought for five decades, an immense political and military pressure that compelled the Sudanese Government in Khartoum to agree to the terms and conditions of the Comprehensive Peace Agreement-2005. The structures and the underlying political ideologies are foreign in nature, but South Sudanese through their quest for independent South Sudan wanted to establish African state, based on African values, and following an african political tradition.

The inception of foreign style of leadership has disturbed and dismembered Africans, and their traditional patrichial rule; the European and the Arabs from the Middle East know that for a fact, nothing stayed African. The West and the Middle East plagued African with what is not theirs, yet they dwelled too much on the foreign civilization. In the deep South, there where greatest rulers, King Gbudwe was one of them, and whose traditional courts and administrative units were very respected, and served the good of their people. When the Anglo-Egyptian administration was installed in Wau, Gbudwe refused to recognize it. Attempts were made twice in 1902-3 from Rumbek and Tonj to occupy his dominion by force but the terrain and good defense saved him.

In 1904, King Gbudwe attacked the Belgians but he was overwhelmed by the machine-gun. He lost many of his men and with them the battle. The British forces troops came in at the

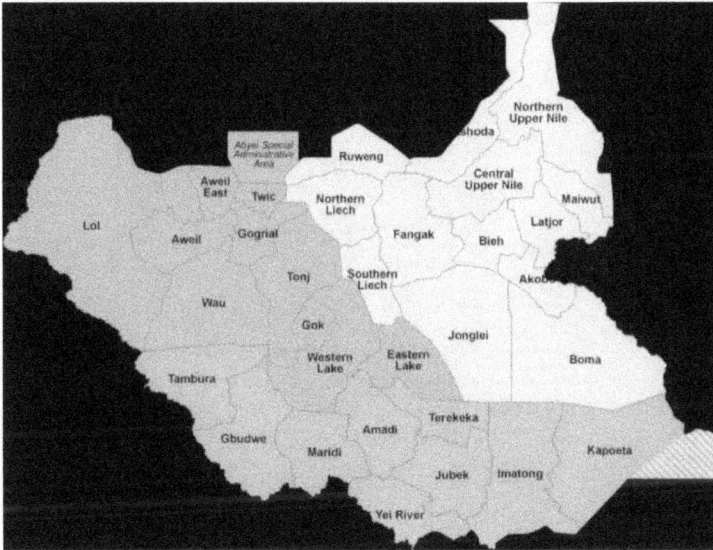

Map South Sudan's 32 states. The Map was adopt on October 2, 2015. It has been published by numerous news outlets including Paanluelwel.com.

beginning of 1905, supported and guided by King Tambura's forces. They met with virtually no resistance. Gbudwe was pursued and killed on 9th of February 1905. Tambura's got what he wanted through betrayal. King Gbudwe was honored in death by his Adversaries. The Anglo-Egyptian firt near his grave was given the name Yambio, which was another name for freedm fighter.[47] Page 15, para.2. South Sudanese at large have political rivalries, and their differences were exploited by colonial

---

47   Alier, Abel. Southern Sudan: Too Many Agreements Dishonoured. New York: Ithaca Press, 1990. In every corner of the old world, indigenous people were colonized based on their local differences. It was the same way that boundaries of what are today refer to as countries were created.

10 STATES + 3 ADMINISTRATIVE AREAS

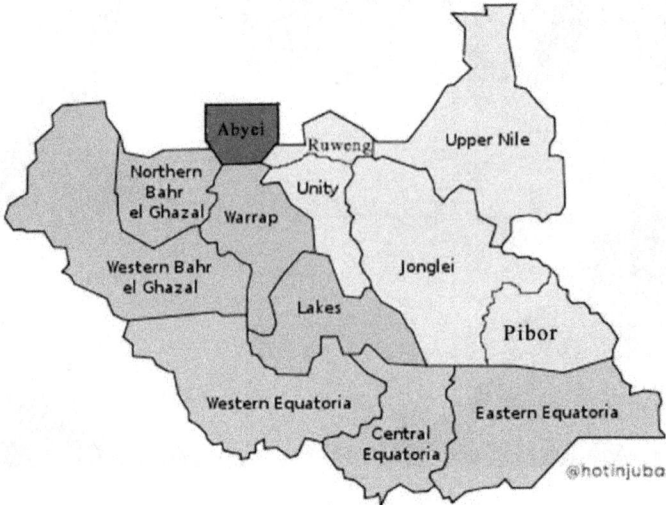

Map by Hot in Juba. This map represents 10 states plus 3 administrative areas decreed by president Salva Kiir Mayardit on February 14, 2020. The new administrative setup was a result of political stalemate between the Government of South Sudan and the SPLM-IO. The Intergovernmental Authority on Development(IGAD) were behind the tough decision by the president.

powers, setting tribes and clans against themselves during the colonial era. The kings and the chiefs were in a constant fight, and that gave both the British and the Arabs-north the opportunity to rule without little resistance from the locals.

Scrambling for Suitable Governance in South Sudan

Shortly after South Sudan plunged itself into political chaos, South Sudan's academics, scholars, and social and political activists went on wild search for a better form of governance in South Sudan. Every newly founded nation does, in its own unique ways, grapple with fundamental issues of governance (Longar Dau, 2016). As suggested by Longar Dau (2016), it is very true that new nations do soul-searching before they settle on what would be the best system to governance themselves, and later run their affairs as they see best fit for their people. However, South Sudan was offline in comparison because 50-years liberation struggle should have been a lesson, a lots have happened in the 5-decades that South Sudanese were fighting the Khartoum based regimes. In the region, and around the world, similar occurrences have availed themselves, and South Sudanese had all the opportunity to prevent certain things from happening.

While debate regarding federalism dated back to pre-independent days, talks intensified when smaller tribes felt overwhelmed by the political gimmicks by the larger tribes, and wanted to find some sorts of balancing mechanism that will make feel at ease. Some started off by suggesting ethnic federalism, a quasi- democratic federal system adopted by the Federal Democratic Republic of Ethiopia and the Republic of Nigeria, claimed to have worked well for multicultural, multiethnic, multilingual and multireligious groups in those countries. Whether people lost the minds in the midst of dusty political turmoil or there is some truth to such search, it remain to been seen in the future. Although people who proposed ethnic federalism do not have full of federalism as a form of governance, the underlying reason was decentralization of powers, something that would give powers local; and create a leverage when in comes to lands issues and what can or cannot be done by the central government.

It can be easily traced back that South Sudanese have had fierce power struggles among themselve, often involved working against everyone's interest. As history reveals, there have been many instances where leaders who stood up for the rights of citizens have been reportedly stabbed at the back.Adversarial deals were initiated at the expenses of the civil population. The whole situation changed when literacy reached some remote areas, and people's political ambition amplified.

The most recent power struggles among South Sudanese are: (a). Political difference within the ranks of the Anya-nya II command, (b). Power struggle within the SPLM/SPLA, followed by the split of 1991, and (c). Political differences between South Sudan's President, Salva Kiir Mayardit, and his longest serving vice president, Dr. Riek Machar in 2013, and over the chairmanship of the SPLM. The President of the Republic fired his Vice President (Dr. Riek Machar) in July 2013, and immediately dissolved the entire Government. At this juncture, the skeptics started to question whether South Sudan's means much to the populace. In 2013, the framing of South Sudan's new independent state as a success story came to an end with the explosion of large-scale ethno-political violence and the beginning of a new civil war (de Simone, 2018). Well, no doubt, South Sudan's independence was a success story, and it is still a success story despite the odd rundowns.

The erratic actions by national leaders plunged the country into irreversal poltical turmoil, the ideology behind independent South Sudan remains intact. The friction aomong the political leaders was rather an opportunity for underground groups who were opposed to the government of the day to sharpen their pangas and join the ranks of oppositions. The two men showcased their political rivalry by criticizing themselves openly like they don't share the same office. The whole drama was an onset of what later became an allout war. No doubt in the minds of people who have been following South Sudan's political and military crises, pres. Salva Kiir and his vice pres. Dr. Riek Machar were returning South Sudan to volatility of the 1990s.

The ingriednts of what became the most devastating in East Africa brewed slowly; not even regional powers nor the international players saw the storm coming. Few months into the conflict, the situation regrettably deriorated, millions displaced internally while other fled to neighbring countries. If recalled properly, power struggle within the ranks and the files of South Sudanese leaders have always led to massive lost of lives, and enormous property damage. There have been no reparations apart from Peace Accords that calmed down the general public.

Nation in the Hands of Significant Others

South Sudan was plunged in political and military crisis due to inability to safeguard its interest, particularly the fossil fuel Reserve that neighbors and signifcants see as their. South Sudan's weakness vis-à-vis foreign actors undermines the legitimacy of the leadership on all sides of the political divide (Rolandsen, 2015, p. 166).[48] The witing impacts of corruption, and political matruirty of the nation's top leaders attracted investors from around the world, and their first glimpse of the newest society sealed off what would been a pure investment. From all that followed, the international corporations and banking institutions begun to make deal with military leaders and nation's lawmakers, and offshore their wealths to far places. The South Sudanese general public, and because of their lack of understanding of what belongs to civil servants, militaty, and politicians made easy for connmen from the Region to setup Ponzi schemes to defraud the civil population of what was truly theirs.[49]

In the dawn of of the South Sudan's independence, there were no mechanisms in place to protect nation's natural wealth,

---

48   Rolandsen, Øystein H. (2015) Another civil war in South Sudan: the failure of Guerrilla Government? Journal of Eastern African Studies 9(1):163-174, DOI:10.1080/17531055.2014.993210

49   The Profiteers- Part 3. https://m.youtube.com/watch?v=aKpJs6a563I The Profiteers, a documentary about looting of South Sudan's resources by it leaders has full stories of who own what, where, and the value of such hidden wealths. Part 3 of the Profiteers have the top South Sudan's leaders, and where they have built villas in East African nations.

and none in term of security the borders. Accountability in the public sector became a morning song, and no one cared about moving the country forward. Witin and beyond the borders of South Sudan, people eyed for easy wealth, South Sudanese continued to live in foreign lands, and as refugees while foreigners flocked into the country for business. "The significant others[50]" took charge of the nation's economy as well as security of the country.

The political leaders deemed corruption as an integral part of the world's newest country. Instead of firing the fix, the president and his team of Advisors sought infrastructure building outside Africa, when for China and negotiated a deal that granted Chinese access to crude Oil. According to the glimpse of the Agreement, the president spoke on a Sunday prayers in in Juba, disclosed that the best alternative was to pay foreign constructors with Oil instead of cash.

"We agreed the road from Nadapal all the way to Torit and to Juba and again from Juba down the road to Rumbek and to Wau... We agreed that South Sudan will not pay them any cash but they will come with whatever they have from their money, they build the roads and we give them crude oil... I decided that the infrastructure or whatever that we want to be done by foreign companies has to be done in exchange for crude oil

---

50   In the world of romance, "significant others" literally means those whose relationship tilt the executive decisions or political stances in issues that matter to the society. But in this case of South Sudan, significant others means superpowers whose manpower and economic leverage influence decisions of their mini-Allies in the developing world.

because our people don't want to see money. If they see money, their hands start shaking," said President Salva Kiir Mayardit.[51]

Immediately after the revelation, there was a thundering outburst on the social media, Government's supporters considered such a move as the best way to scale down on corrupt practices. But, average South Sudan political thinkers looked at it as a very thorny way for the people's Government to avoid accountability through outsourcing the essential part of the public trust. Where else can government give its most valuable commodity in exchange for the construction of the main infrastructure? The way South Sudanese elites governed the country; the way young educated citizens have been excluded from decisions-making tells a different narrative. There have been discrepancies of the highest magnitudes seen in South Sudan, before and after independence. The vocal South Sudanese have been either beaten to death or intimidated to the point that many have given up indefinitely.

In majority of the cases noted, national security is invoked by the authorities, not as it is entailed in law, but as a way to expand their personal control over the governed. There have been little cases of the actual national threat apart of sporadic rebellions seens before the independence. The core of what had been happening in South Sudan is political intimidation, orchestrated by those who felt at odd with fundamentals of

---

51   Hellen Achayo(|September 10, 2018| 1:12 pm). South Sudan to pay Chinese road constructors in crude oil. http://www.eyeradio.org/s-sudan-pay-chinese-road-constructors-crude-oil/

existing national laws. Across the board, there is a growth use and misuse of the national security as enshrined in the constitutional law. The term national security can be used in different senses under different circumstances. Strictly speaking, the term refers to the security of the nation (Lumumba, 1989). The State of South Sudan has been in transitional state since independence. The authorities rush to announce national security whenever their political desires are under public scrutiny. This has impeded on freedom of expressions and freedom of press, and it has many drawbacks. People are always in the state of fear, cannot express fresh ideas that can change things in the country. For example, those ideas are not in line with those of the ruling class are pronounce as enemies of the State and are silenced using abstract security language. Like citizens of the neighboring countries, and in the early years of independence, South Sudanese have been living in the shadow of the crude political shrubs.

"The tendency of the government to conceal issues of detention and matters of national security generally in a shroud of mystery lends credence to the assertion that sometimes national security claims are invoked to cover up embarrassment, incompetence, corruption or outright violation of law" (Lumumba, pp. [52]91, 1989).

It was very disingenuous, and still very unfortunate that

---

52   Lumumba, Patrick Otieno (JULY 1989). National Security in the Kenyan legal System. A Thesis for the Degree of Master of Laws in the University of Nairobi. University of Nairobi Research Archive. http://erepository.uonbi.ac.ke/bitstream/handle/11295/11700/Lumumba_National%20security%20in%20the%20Kenyan%20legal%20system.pdf?sequence=1

world's newest nation started on a wrong path, with unacceptable political practices. The nation of South Sudan was on the verge of collapse since its inception. It is a bitter truth that people tries to disregard, but the facts prove this point otherwise. There was nothing under the Sun that South Sudan was going to be stable and prosperous while in the hands of those who looked inward for the same Sudanese policies that led to 50-year conflict with rest of the country, particularly, the South Sudan that started its quest for independence on the 1947 Juba roundtable. The majority who had the absolute powers and resources at thir fingertips rolled the clocked back to the olden days, & still expect peace and tranquility to prevail in the country.

The hypocrites, from all walks of power in the Republic of South Sudan used their tribal bases to exploit the country, swayed national policies toward their select agendas. Speaking from experience, and near the podium, tribal mindset has overshadowed national identity; South Sudanese tribesmen invested much of their energies & locally generated resources on advancing their isolated communities. It has been observed in many occasions that "a number of African countries evidence the 'paradox of plenty', by which deep poverty of the vast majority of the population coexists with abundance of valuable mineral resources—oil, gas, gemstones and scarce industrial minerals (McFerson, 2009).

South Sudan as a oil rich nation in Africa is no exception to the scenario where abundance of natural resources does not equals to wellbeing of the civil population. Despite South Sudan having oil, gold and other minerals, citizens have been going to through hell while the elites are often seen on a getaway in Arab Emirates, China, Thailand, India, America and Europe. In five star hotels in Juba, the residential places for Government's officials, people are heard giggling about vacation in Bahamas, Bangkok, Bombay, Dubai, Los Angeles and New York.

To the dismay of many observers who wished South Sudanese a peaceful coexistence of their hardearned nation; what was a colorful independence has been auctioned off for few silvers. The tribes as the new enemies of the State are struggling to drawn imaginary lines from within the enclosed borders: tribes against tribes, clans against clans, & sections grasping for oxygen. This is mainly a byproduct of self-interest, warlords polarized the world's newest country beyond recognition. The Movement that liberated the country from Arabization and Islamization lost its vision, and mysteriously started to tear itself into pieces. The then comrades became woes, plunged the country into senseless conflict and burned the people's treasures to ashes.

The vast land of South Sudan, civil population and sovereignty are left vulnerable to the well to do neighborhoods; lands-grabbing and incursion into South Sudan's territories are as normal as hunting in a no man's land. Heart for the country comes from social and cultural integration. With so many loopholes in the system, majority of the enlightened youths have been forced to take tribal routes, talk within circles where ideas and visions are pretty much appreciated. Within the limited, but well defined political mode, the situations have created quasi sociopolitical organizations that take care of the supposedly charity works, and make decisions that are political in nature. The brightest young nationalists have retreated to working for the interest of their local communities, leaving the country more like an orphan. That was purely a result of scaring tactics from the groups that used national security to advance their personal interest.

The present political landscape is a no protection no glory, and majority feel more secure when they are with their tribe-men or clan-men. This is a very pathetic way for a multiethnic nation to submerge itself into. Even in the most developed parts of the world; generous South Sudanese directed their resources to community-based organizations. A nation where brightest are considered as threats to the political establishment is deemed to lag behind. What don't educated South Sudanese have that rest of the world have? A waste of the most enlightened Brains is a disservice to the people of South Sudanese. History, to be written from the diaries of the current madness will be regarded more like a fiction. Who in his right mind would exclude educated population from decisions-making?

Leaders' Quest For Unlimited Power

The jubilations that filled the airwaves when the flag was raised in South Sudan is a living memory. There was more thant attaining the independence, world as a world cherished South Sudanese for their attainment of independent South Sudan, and they wished them to manage their country different. With the ehe interconnectedness of the today's world, unlike past decades, South Sudan was presumably in the right hands. placed South Sudan on top. The leaders as the drivers people aspirations and expectations diverted the vision to suit personal security and interests. Instead of starting off where the line started, South Sudanese elites sought adventures and imaginations at the expenses of their fellow citizens. The little known individuals; people who grew up in the midst of the two decades war were not given the opportunity to put their education and experience into practice.

Like any other nation born out of harsh liberation struggle, South Sudan missed the first thread toward economic prosperity and social stability. Those who were envisioned and foretold as the future of the State become carcasses for the wild animals and birds. The leaders; tribal like all other leaders in underdeveloped countries chose their tribal bases as political launching pad. There was absolutely nothing on the plate that showed progress from day one. Jobs and scholarships were clanized, totally based on local kinship, and no one wanted of work for the future of the country, and that of all the South Sudanese generations whom the 50-years conflict with the Sudan proper was to benefit them. The educated were turned into complainers, national by their own choosing become gossip libraries.

Well, South Sudan has created its own history out of the mud; especially from the senseless civil war 2013-2018 where South Sudan's president, Salva Kiir, and his Vice President, Dr. Riek Machar created their conflict within the realm of the Juba-One State's House(the J1). It's was a wild wondering for many people to see South Sudanese being returned wandering that has contributed withering away of South Sudanese cultures, and diminishing of human development in that region of the world. Seven years down the road, the war of 2013 remain as a senseless conflict, even both the competitors recited "senseless war" in many of their speeches. We all wondered, who actually created the war? For many generations to come, the experiences of 2013-2019 will be revisited, and those who have hearts will live through all that in spirit. Unlike other intrastate conflict, South Sudan's civil war is very unique, and people who cooked and fought the war aren't taking responsibility for all that went wrong. The war has bankrupted the country, displaced more people that the Sudan's 1955-1972 and 1983-2005 wars. As witnessed in digital age world, thousands of people were raced to their graves within just few weeks of the violence. At the course of the armed race, mant villages were torched and properties were destroyed in unimaginable way. The warring parties reportedly vicitimized civil population. This is something often used by warring parties for the following reasons.

Civilians' victimization is a wartime strategy that targets and kills (or attempts to kill) noncombatants .... In protracted wars of attrition, civilian victimization is a form of coercion, that is, the attempt to influence an adversary's behavior by manipulating costs and benefits. Specifically, civilian victimization inflicts costs on noncombatants to coerce a government or rebel organization to cease fighting.[53]

Next is to examine and analyze political competition among the South Sudanese political elites, and its subsequent consequences of living to one's gut. Not much can be said about South Sudan, and not about the leaders. Often, we are reminded that political leaders are the laws, and they are ends to the means. Like salt and pepper, South Sudan's leader pretty much depends on closest relatives to move the mountains and fill valleys. One cannot go without seeing cousins, nephews and nieces making up the board of directors in an office. Sometimes, some hold meaningless titles; no assignments nor responsibilities associated with being a directors of manager. The officials without portfolios are not officials per se, but they are cover to protect the person above, be that the president of the Republic, Governor of a given state or minister. With all that, the largest tribes in the country control everything, and their disagreement is a shared responsibility among the South Sudan's tribes.

The South Sudanese leadership, whose composition is drawn from the two largest tribes of Dinka and Nuer, only cast aside their differences provisionally, allowing for a space to front greater national interest amidst the severe simmering ethnic and

---

53   Alexander B. Downes. (2006). Desperate Times, Desperate Measures: The Causes of Civilian Victimization in War. International Security, 30(4), 152–195. https://lopes.idm.oclc.org/login?url=https://search.ebscohost.com/login.aspx?direct=true&db=edsjsr&AN=edsjsr.4137532&site=eds-live&scope=site

political tensions within the strained government.[54]

The drive for political influence in any given society often lead to rivalry among key political elites in any given period of time. This is simply referred to as political competition, and where certain individuals or groups of individuals want to shape the political, socia and economic agendas of the society. In the case of South Sudan, political competition was widespread long before was was a country called the Republic of South Sudan, and long before there was a geographically defined Region called Southern Sudan. History has it that 1947 Juba Roundtable Conference failed because of influetial Southern Sudanese were not ready to push for an automous Southern Sudan, and it happened in the 17-years armed struggle 1955-1972.

In numerous instances, high-ranking officials have been seen competing in their localities even when they serve at the national positions or in the military command posts. This has had impacts on the local popupaltion, and hindered progress in many ways. The unlimited desire of overarching influence at the local level have been seen through South Sudan, people at the national level have aways wanted to see their clans to dominate everything. Of the many recorded political competition is the case of former Khor Fuluth county, and when the two high-ranking Generals staged a political competition in their home area in northern Jonglei.

---

54   Logo MuLukwat, K. H. (2015). Challenges of Regulating Non-International Armed Conflicts - an Examination of Ongoing Trends in South Sudan's Civil War. Journal of International Humanitarian Legal Studies, 6(2), 414.

Why Khor Fulluth/Pigi? The statistical year book uses both names for the same place. The county, which lies just south of the Barh El Ghazal before it reaches the Sobat, was also called Canal because it was the route for the Jonglei canal. The county is home to four Dinka sections: Ruweng, Rut, Thoi and Luac. Two of the leading sons of the area were George Athor (a Luac of Apadang Jieng)) and Gier Chuang(Ruweng-Paweny). George Athor led the SPLA response to the Khartoum-aligned militias in his home area during the 1990s. But he started a rebellion in 2010 after failing to win the governorship of Jonglei, and he died mysteriously the following year. Gier Chuang, another General, was at the time the minister of interior in Juba. Both were high-ranking SPLA insiders, but they apparently had a personal rivalry, which may have played out in the appointment of rival commissioners, rival names for the county and arguments about dividing.[55]

At the end, the two decorated army generals who were caught up in a tit for tat politics lost their minds. It later led to one dead as a result of rebellion, the other own became a victim of political isolation of another political framing. This is how South Sudan started as a nation, and many stories recorded at the course of seven years, 2008-2013 are nerves-wrecking. The Guerrila Movement that fought the war of liberation dubbed itself in abysess that are hard to digest. The cost for freedom equaled the cost of State structuring. Some leaders whoassualts on Government positions have admitted that South Sudan's

---

55   Thomas. (2015, pp. 137-8). South Sudan: A Slow Liberation.

2013 have cost more lives in the shortest time. There have been zerosum game, and it involved South Sudan's political leaders taking country as their Safe, insured against all sorts of disasters.

The leaders accross South Sudan invested much of their energies and time building local powerhouses. Little known to the local people, the statemen run the show without minding about tomorrow, immediate family members of the leaders in question lived a very luxurious lives in East Africa, in the old Sudan, Egypt, an even in the western world where much of the offshored wealths was amassed. It something that will be read in history books, and others would consider recollections as sort of ghost writings. Who in his right mind would write off the country he/she had fought for, for over decades? The experiment of the 21st centuries has been demonstrated in the Republic of South Sudan, and those who would choose to follow the suit are the dumbfounded who cannot believe the journey of the 98 sheep led by unseasoned leader.

Looking at the bigger picture from the vantagepoint, there had been no initiative apart from building one's base. The many South Sudanese who were very observant have clearly seen what went wrong in the local Jiengs' communities in northern Jonglei, particularly the Luach, Paweny, Rut and Thoi of former Khorfuluth county. Counting on their extended influence in the military, each high-ranking military officer shouldered huge responsibilities toward his own clan. Below is a similar take of what went wrong in Khorfuluth, and narrated by Dr. Peter Adwok Nyaba, a learned South Sudanese known to have offered objective account of political development, both in the liberation struggle as well as in the Govenrment of South Sudan.

The first line of conflict between the political and military elite arose on the basis of where to place boundary and seat of the new county headquarters. For example, the competition for power and influence between Hon. Gier Chuang Aluong and Major General George Athor Deng- re-translated as the Luach-Paweny conflict- could have been old scars rekindled, but the immediate cause was over where to place their county headquarters and through whose political influence that would be achieved. Many lives were lost, yet the two leaders maintained their positions in GOSS and in the SPLA respectively, each attracting friendship of the SPLM chairman and commander in chief of the SPLA, Gen. Salva Kiir Mayardit.[56] (Nyaba, 2016, p. 87).

Poltiical Challenges in the African's State

In South Sudan, lack of enough politically seasoned people makes it possible for semi-literate to take advantage of the masses, design messages that fit their political interests, and let their uninformed citizens act as if they understand the content of the neatly framed political message. In the first few years of the conflict that erupted in Juba on December 15, 2013, some young South Sudanese who supported the Government and those who supported the SPLM-IO decided to pull back to their localities, designed things that fit their interests and impeded on the peace that was being negotiated in Addis Ababa, Ethiopia.

---

56   South Sudan: The State We Aspire To. (2016, 2nd Edition). Africa World Books Pty Ltd. 2nd Edition

Some of the things seen after the independence can all be credited to unpreparedness of the country to govern itself. It was not by accident that South Sudan plunged itself into endless cycle of tribal conflicts; big part of the problem has a lot to with South Sudan's institutional failure to adapt and adept to challenges of running a modern State. In keeping up with academic recollection of the 21st century political literature piping, one the Africa's news and media house, The Citizen (2020) had this to say about the Republic of South Sudan:

"The liberators, typical of how they undermined their own revolution all across Africa, were not going to relinquish any space for the country's other types of human capital to contribute to the shaping of the country's development. It was these liberation fighters who were now to become the administrators, bank officials, police officers, judges, accountants and human resource personnel, after two decades of very little to no exposure to systems of governance of any kind. Most of them had no capacity to do the jobs they now occupied. But the mention of this was near taboo. They were the ones to set up the institutions of the new state and the whole endeavor of state-building, of bringing professionalism to the institutions, strengthening the rule of law and entrenching the philosophy and practice of state machinery, faltered. This is not to say the failure of the state is entirely the fault of liberators."[57]

Across South Sudan, there were countless posters that were displayed in public rallies, photographed and posted on the

---

[57]   The Citizen (Dar Es Salaam, Tanzania) - AAGM. (2020). Exposing South Sudan governance failure. https://lopes.idm.oclc.org/login?url=https://search.ebscohost.com/login.aspx?direct=true&db=edsgao&AN=eds-gcl.640096905&site=eds-live&scope=site&custid=s8333196&groupid=-main&profile=eds1

social media for supporters to read, and possibly to propagate propagandas online. Such tactics prolonged the war, and at the same time made it difficult for the opposing leaders to follow through with path recommended for them by the Inter-Governmental Authority on Development (IGAD), the Troika and the international community. As soon as the war breaks out in any political volatile country, leaders whose conflicting interests lead to fighting do not hold the key to cessation of hostilities. It truly became the case when the disagreement within the SPLM as a ruling party exploded, a President Salva Kiir and his former vice President, Dr. Riek Machar were no longer in total control of people fighting on the streets and the bushes of South Sudan. The message of war spilled to villages, and people who have cases against the Government thought they have a reason to take up arms against the Regime, leave their cattle camps and marched toward to Juba, ransacking villages and burning shops in the towns they passed through.

In just two weeks, much of the Jonglei, Upper Nile and Unity state were war zones, and corpses were lying everywhere. That did not end there, some political dissidents in other 7 states of South Sudan sneaked out of the country and joined members of SPLM-IO at the South Sudan-Ethiopia border. The war raged, millions displaced from their homes and promising nation's future was disgracefully compromised in less than three months. There were of course numerous avenue for South Sudanese to contain the conflict, but instead, leaders dusted off the possibility for diffusing the tension. Those who sought military solution were obviously wrong, and the records for damages done speak loudly. The rebels had inner fighting, which gravely cost them a considerable chunks of the objectives against the Government in Juba.

Violence is South Sudanese

Ethnic politics is irrational, distracting, apolitical and averse to nation building and national integration. No patriot should ever entertain the idea of a short cut to power through the politicization of ethnicity or the ethnicization of politics.[58](Nyaba, 2016, pp. 87).

The unresolved issues of the SPLM and SPLA converged in 2013, coming to a head over the preparations for 2015 Presidential election. With the top leadership of the SPLM there was a large constituency in favor of reform and specific challenge by the Vice President, Riek Machar, for the party's nomination for president (Johnson, 2016, p.176). South Sudanese as the indigenious people of the SUDAN have their past to close to them in many respects. In the olden days, authority was pretty much supported by ability to hold power, and uses violence to have a firm grip on it. Dinka-Nuer ethnic groups elites' rivalry for power using ethnicity as a mobilizing force and the resultant animosity that has characterized the two ethnic groups relations and often caused ethnic atrocities in all sides (Tekalign,

---

58   South Sudan: The State We Aspire To. (2016, 2nd Edition). Africa World Books Pty Ltd. People often condemn tribal politics, but they appear to do the exact opposite. There have been instances whereby critics of such politics have criticized based on their own tribal indifferent. Only generations to come would differentiate which is which, if actually people meant what they said or wrote.

Map 3. Approximate territories of principal ethnic groups in the Upper Nile Region (ca. 1983).

Map showing major ethnic Groups in South Sudan. Hutchinson, Sharon E. Nuer Dilemmas: Coping with Money, War, and the State. University of California Press, 1995. In the areas shown above, the communites identified are the political playersin South Sudan, and have historical records for racing themselves to demise.

2015).[59] It has been well documented throughout the centuries that these tribes (Dinka and Nuer) are engaged in a militaristic dealing. Whenever there is a disagreement between these tribe, the civil population suffer badly.

59   Tekalign, Yohannes. (2015). Challenges for Peace in South Sudan: Problems and opportunities of solving the current civil war. International Researchers (4)2, https://www.academia.edu/14186302/CHALLENGES_FOR_PEACE_IN_SOUTH_SUDAN_PROBLEMS_AND_OPPORTUNITIES_OF_SOLVING_THE_CURRENT_CIVIL_WAR

The history of violence and physical confrontation among the South Sudanese tribes is straightforward. It has been noticed that leaders use their positions to protects interests of their subordinates. And they use unquestionable physical power to protect lands and resources in their proximity. In many instances, tribes in cattle rearing communities fight over pastures and water, and that often results into animals being snatched from their rightful owners. Such wars still exist till these days; children, elderly and women are the primary victims of such rivalries.

The natives recall their leaders through the kinds of things they have done; heavy causalties on rival communities is never missing from they stories, and with not much change in social and political structures, they same mindset have been carried down to the independent South Sudan, and all of there is responsible for awful violence conflict that erupted on December 15, 2013. As observed by Evans-Pritchard, and who spent a considerable amount of times among the Nuer and the Azande people of South Sudan, he wrote very detailed notes about his anthropological works in the SUDAN. Like rest of the researchers around the Globe, Evans-Pritchard observed that bravery, and in the form of physical violence is not separable from what a person live for.

As Nuer are very prone to fighting, people are frequently killed... A Nuer will at once fight if he considers that he has been insulted, and they are very sensitive and easily take offense... From their earliest years, children are encouraged by their elders to settle all disputes by fighting, and they grow up to regard skill in fighting the most necessary accomplishment and courage the highest virtue (Evans-Pritchard, 1940, p. 151).[60]

This is true about all the pastoral South Sudanese communities, and the main reason behind wreckless killing of citizens across South Sudan since the inception of Autonomous
Government of Southern Sudan in 2005. Everything appeared
to surfaced after the Region was granted a self-rule, but truth to
the matter is that tribe in South Sudan have been like that for
the past centuries. In the first few of war in Juba (2013), people
used a tribal rhetorics that helped mobilized fighters on both
sides of the political divides, disgruntled political stooges used
tribal political cards to narrow chances of stopping the war.
Only a well crafted education, economic, political and social
programs can change the way tribes live their lives, and they go
about their normal daily activities without causing harms onto
their fellow South Sudanese.

The marginal standoff cannot just stop without an inputs
from authroties in South Sudan. The Government in South
Sudan has not made strategic planning to change pragmatic
way of life in South Sudan, and where tribes see themselves
as enemies rather than being one people with common goal.
Some ruthless militias commanders have been rewarded by the
Government of President Salva Kiir for accepting amnesty while
their militias remained at large, and pursuing the cattle rustling
across tribal-ethnic borderlines. The disorientated tribal elites
have invested much of their political life in their tribes and all
the local stuffs thatn make them so special. This abhorrence of

60   Evans-Pritchard, E.E. The Nuer: A description of the Modes of Livelihood and Political Institutions of a Nilotic People. Oxford University Presss, 1940.

tribalism in South Sudan has emerged from the rise in nationalism in 2011, when the country became independent following a series of conflicts (Sano, 2019).

The prime example of a tribal warlord who secured himself a post in Kiir's government is David Yau Yau of the South Sudan Democratic Movement-Cobra Faction. Rule of law does not exist in a a vacuum, a government of the day has to put in place some mechanism that stop certain groups from disturbing peace. The African traditional society have one thing in common; the smaller and the weaker ones have always been at the mercy of the richest and the most power. Back in the day, tribes in the Upper Nile Region of the Sudan were often raided, and queezed to the edge by the Nuer. The British aministration by then created security stations, mainly to protect ethnic communities from aggressive and violent neighbors.The followed was one of the many initiatives:

The Kongor post was opened in December 1908 to protect the Dinka(Jieng) from Nuer and Beir(Murle) raids. On April 27, 1909, a second station was opened farther north at Duk Fadiet where provincial boundaries between Mongalla and Upper Nile Provinces had been agreed to follow the frontier between the Dinka and Nuer tribal territories. But in enforcing this segregation, the government entered into conflict with the Nuer who were expected to move out of occupied Dinka land. Some resisted expulsion, culminating in the Lau attack on Duk Fadiet in June 1910 before they were finally moved out of Mongalla Province in 1911 and their leader arrested. Owen's active intervention in traditional tribal conflicts escalated the violence. Warfare continued between the Dinka and Nuer; Beir raids on the Bor Dinka became more frequent, striking four times in two years between 1909 and 1910.The Gawaar and Ghol/Hol continued to raid each other, with the warrior sons of Deng Laka, Macar and Wol, being killed in 1914 by Ghol (Hol Dinka/Jieng). In 1916 the Lau raided deep into the Bor Dinka country to within a few miles of the district headquarters of Bor, and the government, unable to control the raids, had to distribute rifles to the Dinka at Kongor and Duk Fadiet to enable them to withstand the Nuer.[61]

Jieng at the Center of South Sudan's Polity

The tribe called Jieng, also known as Dinka by foreigners has been at the center of Sudanese and South Sudanese politics for many decades before the split of the African largest country. The Jieng coauthor the popular conference whwich came to be known as 1947 Juba Roundtable. As one of the largest tribes in the then Sudan, and the most populous tribe in South Sudan, it has enjoyed both the privilege and suffered the greatest loss in terms of humans. The exterminations that took place between 1962 and 1972 targeted mostly Jiengs in the Greater Barh El Ghazal and the Greater Upper Nile.

The chiefs in the Upper Nile were massacred for allegedly supporting the Anyanya Movement, and it followed the 1967

---

61   Mawut, Lazarus Leek (1995, p.85-6). The Southern Sudan under British Rule 1898-1924 : the constraints reassessed., Durham theses, Durham University. Available at Durham E-Theses Online: http://etheses.dur.ac.uk/971/

Malakal conferences where the head chiefs demanded a regional government to be established in the South, based in Juba to deliver services to the Sudanese in the lower part of the country. During the two wars of liberation, both Anyanya Movement, and the Sudan People's Liberation Movement/Army. It's of course known that guerrilla warfare results into many deaths, especially the invading groups, mostly the rebels trying to topple the government of the day.

The South Sudanese struggle against Khartoum successive regimes was no exception, the South Sudanese received material supports from those afar and logistics was provided by the local. But targeting chiefs was unwise decision by the Sudanese Government, it later grown in size, and subsequently led to the partition of the country. The harsh treatment of the South Sudanese amplified in the years that followed, and later generation picked up the fight, and fought aggressively against the Sudanese Government, establishing a strong armed rebelled in Africa. The war attracted World's superpowers, and all played on an opposite sides.

Long history of violence in South Sudan

The trumucious tribal and interethnic/inter communal conflicts has so much to do with traditional polity. South Sudan has seen unprecedented killing in the last 10 years, tribal and ethnic lines have been more of a Death Valleys. Quite a considerable number of youths have been killed in senseless violence; children, elderly and women subjected to unbearable suffering.

Political factors are also important in explaining ethnic conflicts. In countries with democratic governments, people have equal representation in politics. Discrimination and exclusionary ideologies are not acceptable. In countries with authoritarian regimes, not all ethnic groups are treated similarly. When oppression and discrimination are used by the government against one group, there is little doubt that it will lead to internal conflict. Violence is more likely to happen when the ethnic groups are ambitious for power and have strong ethnic identities. Opportunistic politicians take advantage of political instability and economic turmoil to divert attention from the real problems besetting the country.[62]

The Government, crippled by tribal mindset and unprepared officials have not done much to maintain law and order. It shocked the world how a country founded on quest for freedom turned against itself within first few years of independence. The South Sudanese civil population have not had time to enjoy the 50-years struggle against the successive governments in Khartoum. It was a blink of an eye, and South Sudanese could be seen running away from themselves; Khartoum, and other regions became hiding places.

The war in South Sudan, like any nation the world took a complicated dimension. As warring parties engaged in violence, there were some foreign interests that propelled the warring parties to cause more destructions to their country. Instead of open state to state warfare, nation-states often use and support

---

62   Tepfenhart, M. (2013). The Causes of Ethnic Conflicts. Comparative Civilizations Review, 68, 84–97. https://lopes.idm.oclc.org/login?url=https://search.ebscohost.com/login.aspx?direct=true&db=ofs&AN=87591213&site=eds-live&-scope=site&custid=s8333196&groupid=main&profile=eds1

sub-national or extra-national armed organizations to work against enemies. This type of conflict is known as proxy war (Auerbach, 2021).[63] There has been an ongoing war proxy war in South Sudan as nations with vested interests in South Sudan's oil reserve and minerals supported and continue to give supports to sides that are opposed to by their economic competitors. There is now, as there has been throughout the 20th century, a complete absence of any effective global authority capable of controlling or settling armed disputes. Globalization has advanced in almost every respect - economically, technologically, culturally, even linguistically - except one: politically and militarily, territorial states remain the only effective authorities (Hobsawm, 2002).[64]

The vast land of South Sudan was left for wildlife and foreigners who ceased the opportunity to make money in a volatile environment. With many witnesses on the ground, foreign entrepreneurs and investors are more secure than South Sudanese returning from the developed world or the developing countries in the Middle East. The vision of the SPLM flipped; only very few within the ruling elites remember what the call for independent South Sudan was all about. The towering figures of the liberation movement have chosen to spend much of the remaining time

63   Auerbach, M. P. (2021). Global Politics: Causes of War. Salem Press Encyclopedia. https://lopes.idm.oclc.org/login?url=https://search.ebscohost.com/login.aspx?direct=true&db=ers&AN=89185503&site=eds-live&scope=site&custid=s8333196&groupid=main&profile=eds1
64   Hobsawm, E. (2002, February 23). War and peace. The Guardian. Retrieved November 22, 2021, from https://www.theguardian.com/education/2002/feb/23/artsandhumanities.highereducation

not talking about the importance of keeping people intact, developing the country, reconciling communities at war and so forth.

On the far end of the political fulcrum, the youth who had the energy to change the country have aged doing social and political activism, and all the efforts and peace's advocacy felt on deaf ears. For one, the State initiated a program that tracked down writers and Human Rights Activists, arrest them and subject them harsh treatment. Since 2012, the national apparatuses, supposedly for the safety and security of South Sudan doubled up trivial- thin lines stuffs, and unapologetically amassed resources and directed unseasoned agents to do the unthinkable. Well, that is how the third world don't move an inch.

The history of violence and tribal rivalry in the South Sudanese society dated back to the colonial period. South Sudanese tribes are known in the history as very violence, they raided themselves in the past, abducted children and women and children, and displaced their own people are the course of fighting land, water and pastures. This intensified when the automaticed weapons were introduced, and a considerable number of people become schooled. The select people who had access to education seized the opportunity to influence political processes in their home villages, became vocal advocate for social justice, and started to compete among themselves to the point that they reopened the old wounds. The liberation struggle that gave birth to the Republic of South Sudan experienced political turbulences, and quite a number of South Sudanese sons who joined the Movement perished in a mysterious manner. Below is how the South Sudanese society looked like in the pre-colonial and in the colonial periods:

The governor of Mongalla Province which shared a border with Upper Nile Province, took the very opposite view to that of Matthews with regard to maintaining peace among warring tribes... Owen went to Mongalla with a policy of aggressive territorial expansion. It has already been seen that the Governor General had to issue harsh instructions to curb Owen's expansionist tendencies. Owen's policy was to be achieved through extending government protection against local adversaries to loyal government tribes which paid taxes. To be protected were the Bor, Twic, Nyarweng and Ghol Dinka against Beir (Murle) and Nuer raids. Until 1912 the Beir were still outside government control, while the Nuer were in Matthews' province. Owen had already in June 1908 persuaded the Central Government to despatch a military force against the Beir in retribution for their raid on the Bor Dinka. His orders to the officer commanding the Beir Patrol were specific: the tribe 'must be punished and made to feel it; and to realise once for all that they cannot raid another tribe with impunity'. For immediate occupation was the Twic, Nyarweng and Ghol country north of the Bor Dinka. These tribes shared borders with the Zeraf and Lau Nuer. Owen wanted to open stations in the area to offer the Dinka protection against Nuer raids. He accordingly pressed the Central Government to allow him to establish a station at Kongor, giving as justification what he saw as a desperate security situation in the area.[65]

Jieng is a Dominance Political Force

The policy of "divide and rule" by the Sudanese Government gave birth to a United Jieng, and strengthened the SPLM/ SPLA. With the birth of the South Sudan, majority of the army officers in top positions were Jiengs, and well nurtured in military affairs. The setup of the new State was not so smooth because the untimely passing on of Dr. John Garang de Mabior as the President of the Government of Southern Sudan, First Vice President of the Sudan, Chairman of the SPLM and Commander-in-chief of the SPLA complicated and compromised what would have been a smooth transition into Statehood. It can be easily sensed from the decade long mourning by South Sudanese leaders. People in position in power kept crying of having missed John Garang, that is incapable they become in the most of vulnerable South Sudanese.

The new structures in the military and the states' government shifted the central command that was known by many. When

---

65   Mawut, Lazarus Leek (1995, pp.84-5). The Southern Sudan under British Rule 1898-1924 : the constraints reassessed., Durham theses, *Durham University*. Available at Durham E-Theses Online: http://etheses. dur.ac.uk/971/ - More than a century later, not much has changed as far as the security situation is concern in South Sudan. The tribes in much of South Sudan are still engaging in violence, raiding cattle and abducting children. The Government, even after South Sudan became an independent country has not done something to break the cycle of violence. Politics and personal interests have reduced leaders into stooges of greed.

dust started to settle, most people, particular junior SPLA's commanding officers began to disperse into semi-military life, leaving a wide vacuum in the security sectors. The merging of South Sudanese who were in Sudanese Army and those who were in the SPLA introduced another element of confusion. In between, Jiengs occupied most of the Government institutions, and other minority South Sudanese ethnicities see them left out. The center was more of all same faces, and the mistrust started to flourish. The civil society organizations that pushed for equitable running of what would be a country were demurred by the unseasoned security organ, some disappeared in mysterious way, some arrested and others prosecuted for reporting on Government. All these created a situation where the South Sudan's largest tribes; Jieng and Naath became the Irons of the new State.

It's also worth mentioning that Naath/Nuer shared a lot with Jieng, but because of the crisis of the early 1990s, there was a great suspicion within the files and ranks of the military. Therefore, Naath officers chickened out, chose to be at the receiving end, and put in little effort to partake in the structuring of the country. When politics boiled, and reached an evaporation point, there were not muscles left for others to challenge the leadership of the Jieng's president, and he did everything in his power to remain as the chairman of the ruling party, commander-in-chief of armed forces.

Power Vacuum!

The most triguing thing is passes of leaders who have dominated every aspect of the society, and where there is no much
preparation put in place for the next generation of leaders to
take charge of the country's affairs. In the South Sudanese societies, when leaders vanishes, from natural death or in the hands
of their opponents, the society suffers a blowback. It can be
easily said that such drawbacks are the result of a society lacking
central authority. The absence of a nationalistic figures to close
the gap and phrepherical mindsets play into the narrative. With
the untimely of Dr. John Garang de Mabior, a lot worse took
place in the eyes of so many people who were once revered by
the South Sudanese and other marginalized Sudanese. There
is nothing hallow than leaving an aspiration of the people to
leader who is not prepared to face the world. Long before the
SPLM/SPLA signed a Peace Agreement with Sudanese Government in Khartoum, Southern Sudanese, both in the bushes of
Southern Sudan and in the northern part of the Sudan wanted
to topple Dr. John Garang by all possible means.

The most lethal failed attempt to oust Garang from the
Liberation Movement occurred in 1991 when Dr. Riek Machar,
Dr. Lam Akol and Cdr. Gordon Kong Chol staged coup against
their chairman of the SPLM/SPLA. The whole situation was
quickly exploited by the enemy in Khartoum, and started to
buy some of the splinter Groups the bushes. As a result of the
power struggle fromwithin, the Movement was hit really hard,
lost major garrison towns to the Sudanese armed Forces and

militias that were allied to the Regime in Khartoum. That left the SPLM/SPLA to be on life-support, up until when some Regional players leaned hands to its, and helped in driving the Sudanese army to northern part of Southern Sudan. Despite that, the SPLM/SPLA held its morale intact, and garnished an international supports, and pinned down the Sudanese Government on Human Rights violations.

The world at large sympathized with the Sudanese people, and a grand peace Accord was cheerished by Churches and Human Rights organizations. When Dr. John Garang was no more, and the independent South Sudan continued to be at the mercy of Government in Khartoum, those who once thought Garang's leadership was the worse came to termed with his outstanding performance in the midst of the African longest running civil war. To destabilize South Sudan, the Sudanese Kharotum continued armed tribes to fight themselves, fitting cattle keepers against cattle keepers. Across South Sudan, many communities depends on their livestocks; often use as medium of exchange, pay as dowry to many cases. Cattle had social agency as beings in their own right, and also through their abilities or potential abilities to circulate through society, establishing and maintaining relationships (King, 2017).

With the breakdown of the Government's institutions, there have been a power vacuum, and local take laws into their own hands. The lack of government presence in these areas constitutes a trigger for criminal operatives to operate with impunity (Olaniyan, & Yahaya, 2016). The Government of the Republic of South Sudan has underperformed far below the performances of the SPLM/

SPLA during the war of liberation. Criminality surrounding cattle in itself can have national security implications (Cline, 2020). The SPLM in the bush was more effective than the SPLM as the ruling party in the Republic of South Sudan. What is very clear in all these is whoever in the driver's seat matters the most. Here is a testimony from the ironman, Dr. Peter Adwok Nyaba:

Without doubt, Gen. Salva Kiir Mayardit is different from his predecessor, Dr. Garang, in everything-from leadership style, etiquette and diplomacy to the capacity to endure long hours of hard work. With Garang, it was clear there was somebody in the driving seat of every process in the SPLM/SPLA. It was certain that there would always be decisive measures taken for any situation, with nothing left to chance.[66]

Political Gimicks

Different account of December 15, 2013
Heroes of South Sudan: David De Dau

The revelation below is one of the many stories picked up by humanitarian organizations, and used it to build their case of a grand Human Rights violations.

"My compound had never been so full of people but I understood the need for people to find a safe space. My home is considered safe because I am a Dinka."David De Dau

---

66   Nyaba, Peter Adwok (2016, p.130). South Sudan: The State We Aspire To. Dr. Peter AdwokNyaba is known for criticizing leaders in every stage, and without taking a second chance for his observations. He has written extensively on the Sudanese and the South Sudanese political affairs in the past 20 years.

While we need to investigate and make public all violations of human rights in the South Sudan crisis, we also need to shed light on the many people who went above and beyond to help those from ethnic groups different from their own. These are the voices of those who went the extra mile. Their bravery and strength in light of the situation they faced is a testament to the extraordinary power of compassion, hope and the will to survive. David De Dau, 38, lives in Gudele, Juba. Here is how he experienced the outbreak of violence: On Sunday 15th December 2013, I arrived in Juba after a long drive from Gulu, Uganda. At around 8:30 pm, I heard gunshots from the Giada where the Presidential Tiger Guards were based. I got a call immediately after from a friend who worked with national security, telling me to stay put. I was shocked because I didn't know that South Sudanese people could still take up arms against each other. Two days after the fighting started, I had to collect my mother-in-law from Miahusaba area. As I drove back, I was stopped by some policemen on the road. I reduced my speed to a snail's pace and rolled down the glass window. Police officer dressed in uniform: "Maale?" They asked, meaning peace be with you in Nuer.

Peace is good "Maalemugwa," I responded. Peace is good. This was obviously the wrong response as they cocked their guns at me and ordered me to get out and fall to my knees. "Get him, he's Nuer." My mother-in-law wanted to scream saying he is not Nuer, I ask her to keep quiet. I got out of the car slowly and stood at the front right-side of my car. As they were about to shoot, I opened my mouth to speak. What were a few minutes of running my mouth going to cost me if I was going to die? I had a few chosen words for them. This time I chose to speak in Dinka, my native language. The surprise on their faces was priceless. I will never die on my knees "I am not going on my knees. Feel free to shoot but I will never die on my knees." Bold, I know, but they did not shoot. I proceeded.

"If you had asked me in Arabic 'Salaam Aleikum', I would have responded in Arabic saying 'Aleikum Salaam'. Would that mean that I am an Arab? If you can answer that convincingly, then I am now ready to die." They dropped their guns and looked at me intently, then at each other. "Where are you from?" they asked. Bold with the presence of life in my body, I decided to provoke them further. "Why do you want to know? Why is it so useful for you to know where I hail from?" I asked. "Just tell us where you're from," he repeated, now visibly irritated.

"I roughly speak five languages, so I am from five different places," I said. "You, give us your ID!" I'm a free citizen of South Sudan" I left it at home. And even if I had it, what reason do you have for asking for it. Am I not a free citizen of South Sudan?" I asked, now also visibly irritated. I did leave my house for a reason and this was not it. "Give us your Driving License!!!" I did. They could not read. They handed it back to me and told me that if I was moving around and wanted to stay alive, I should reveal where I am from and speak my language. Not everyone would be as patient as they were to me." My people have shot me." My cousin had lost his life the same way only a few days before. He had responded in Arabic and before he could finish a sentence, he was on his way out. "My people have shot me," were his last words in Dinka. The man who had pulled the trigger then dropped his gun and started crying. He had killed one of his own. The irony is not lost on me. My mother-in-law and I drove to my house in silence. Sometimes there is so much to say but no one willing to say it. No one stopped the car this time. We reached home safe.

My compound had never been so full of people but I understood the need for people to find a safe space. My home is considered safe because I am a Dinka. What does safety mean I reflect on this as I say hello to my Nuer neighbors and their children who I have hidden in my house. How safe it is, I don't know. I am considered safe but I was almost killed today based on flawed logic. I am considered safe, yet people constantly stalk my compound asking for "the Nuer" that live in the compound next to mine. I remember one visit clearly. "We know there are Nuer people who live in the houses next door. Do you know where they are?" they asked. "I don't know where they are, they probably ran to the camp." "Ok, then we will do something else to send a message," they said, walking to their houses with every intention to loot and destroy. "Those houses belong to me. I am renting them to the Nuer neighbors you are looking for. If you destroy them, you are destroying my property. What message are you trying to send to me because you can just tell me now." They left. I wonder if I'd still be considered safe if they know that the people they were looking for were in my house."[67]

---

[67] South Sudanese in South Sudan blamed diasporas for detailed account of ethnic targeting. https://www.oxfam.org/en/emergencies/heroes-south-sudan-david-de-dau

In much of the rural South Sudan, communities have conflicts that dated back to Stone Age period. Cattle rustling
are presumably a way of life to some tribes. For example, the
Murles of Jonglei are known for raiding their neighbors' cows
and abducting children. The practice is absurd and barbaric
from the outside world, but the Murle themselves including
the schooled ones deemed it as their way of life. In the last fifty
years, especially with South Sudanese wide access to the outside
world, the Murle's practice of raiding cattle, burning down villages, depriving parents of their children has been condemned,
termed by Humans Rights watchdogs as a modern day slavery.
The attempts by both the Sudanese Government before in of
South Sudan failed. The Sudanese Government during the war
of liberation armed the Murle to the teeth, used them as para-
military to suppress the rebellion in the South Sudan. When
Southern Sudan was granted Autonomous Government by the
Comprehensive Peace Agreement (CPA) signed between the
Sudanese Government in Khartoum and the SPLM/SPLA, the
Regional Government in Juba did little to eradicate the practice.

In 2010, and on the first ever election in Southern Sudan
since the war broke out in 1983, an aspirant for the state's assembly seat, by the name of David YauYau, a Murle by ethnicity
took up arms against the Juba based Autonomous Government.
His reasons, as he later explained in serious of interviews claimed
his win having been stolen by his Rival, Jody Jonglei. The new
War farther the Murle's archaic way of life, and Murle's of the
South Sudan Democratic Movement-Cobra Faction raided
Jieng's villages in Jonglei, killing scores, displacing thousands,

abducting hundreds of children, and looted tens of thousands heads of cattle.

The Murle's raiding did not stop with Jiengs in Jonglei, the hungry thugs crossed into Ethiopia in 2014, raided cattle and goats in Western Ethiopia. The Savannah thugs burned down villages, and abducted hundreds of children. The Ethiopian Government responded by sending troops into South Sudan, military helicopters were sent across the borders, and Murle's Chiefs were instructed to returned the abducted children and stolen cows or face Ethiopian military. The response was very promising, majority of the children abducted were recovered and returned to their relatives in western Ethiopian. In other parts of South Sudan such as Eastern Equatoria, cattle rustling were very common up until the mid-2000.

There has been a very strategic shift in the way violence and cattle-rustling has been frequent states in Bahr El Ghazal. Majority of the people who rear cattle in Bahr El Ghazal (Lakes, Warrap, Northern Bahr El Ghazal and Western Bahr El Ghazal) are Dinkas. The way youths have been engaged in cattle theft is shocking. Not that cattle-rustling was unheard, but the pro-lifieration of small arms, and lousy law enforcement has raised the potential for thieves to raid cattle and get away without being brought to book. For those who are unfamiliar with South Sudan intercommunal conflict, each region has it unique problem, and the phenomenon of cattle-ruslting is reported more like a new thing.

Clashes over resources are common in Warrap state - its six counties have long experienced grave levels of conflict and violence, largely relating to cattle rustling and competition over water points and grazing lands. This volatility is exacerbated by the widespread ownership of arms, which state authorities seem unable to control. Since South Sudan's liberation war, the state has suffered particularly severe strife, including forced migration, instability, the decimation of their property, and fatalities, much of it inflicted from within. Peace has been elusive.[68]

This is not a new thing, the Jiengs/Dinkas in Warrap state do not live in isolation, they have people in neighboring unity state stealing from them as well as Lakes state raiding their cattle. The back and forth raiding of cattle has been an ongoing thing for quite sometimes, but the today's media reporting plus citizens access to medium and forms of communication often dramatize the severity of the cattle-rustling as a violent act. Credit to the people's lifestyle, cattle-rearing communities increase their herds by raiding their neighborhoods. All of these have contributed to absolute poverty and instability in South Sudan. The Government, whether the Sudanese Government in those days or the South Sudanese Government after independence haven't put in place mechanisms that address the unbecoming practices. The areas where tribes raid themselves are not feasible for investment or agricultural production. No sane business person would invest in an environment where people are killed in a broad daylight.

---

68   Spittaels, Steven, & Weyns, Yannick. (2014). Mapping Conflict Motives: the Sudan - South Sudan Border. Academia Letters. https://www.academia. edu/10372816/Mapping_Conflict_Motives_the_Sudan_South_Sudan_Border

Politics of Isolation Through Marginalization

The nation of South Sudan started on a wrong footing; some select groups and tribal-minded allies had a showcase of what they really want to achieve at the expenses of their fellow countryperson. That kind of working along kinship dated back to the olden days where South Sudanese were peasons, and had to rely on their own people to get things done or fight wars of survival. From day one, there was a fierce power struggle among the military elited and political elites of South Sudan. No sane person expected this to go away with input of the enlightnened generation of leaders. The former warlords, graciously known as freedomfighters were not prepared to take on the nation's challenges, all of which include witchhunt from South Sudan's former foes and adversaries. Within just a flipped of a second, the nation of South Sudan was embroiled in acute political wrangles where elites were on the throats.

With so much dependence oil as the leading national treasury in South Sudan; leaders were quick to corner jobs in mining sector, and seured them for the relatives and blindfollowers. Over the years, people have been scrambling for Government's positions, and a lot of political unrest ensued. This involves framing potential rivals and competitors who are more likely to occupy certain positions. As evidenced by the unprecedented rebellion in the country, those who have been pushed of their positions always have things to say, and not everything they say in untruth. Some of the revelations come to surface after people have been fired, replaced or accused of certain misconducts. It's also important to note that those who speak after the acute lose of jobs do it out of frustration because hope is no longer there. The top Government's officials who lost their jobs had something attached to their names. Even Attachés of foreign service have been implicated in politics at home, and either recalled or fired while still abroad.

Duk Panyang & Duk Payuel Massacre on November 27, 2017

The ethnic conflicts in South Sudan has taken a toll on the country. Many attempts to forge coexistence through peace have been a complete failure. In just one week since the Greater Jonglei communities convened inter-communal peace according in Duk Padiet of Duk Region, Raiders from the Murle tribe made coordinated and simultaneous attacks on Duk Panyang and Duk Payuel. The first phase of the attack was November 27, 2017, and at around 4:00 pm South Sudan local time. The fighting raged until 8:00pm with youths hanging on to their carried. Early in the morning, on November 28, 2017, the retreating Raiders diverted to Duk Payuel, some 24 Miles Southwest of Duk Panyang county. The dawn helped the raiders overwhelmed the locals, 42 lives were lost and 56 children and women were taken by the invading Murle's youths.

For the victims of such heinous act, it was apocalyptic in many ways; children, elderly and women were showered down by the marauding raiders who spare no life. There was a small child, 4 months old slaughtered by the attackers. One would not imagine the kinds of values inflated into those young boys. Their mentors have no sense of humanity, have no remorse for the vulnerable and destroyed lives and properties as if they come from another planet.

Warlordism at its Core

After Garang's death, his successor, Salva Kiir, and the remaining leaders of the SPLM paid lip service to the 'New Sudan' vision, but no more. Instead, Kiir and others like Riek Machar turned inwards to concentrate on the politics of the south, rather than those of Sudan.[69]

The nation of South Sudan was founded on democratic principles: Justice, Equality and Freedom of Expression. The country has a Transitional Constituion. These fundamental principles, though enshrone in the Constitution only exist in abstract. The cores have been abused by the warlords who rose to the ranks during the war of liberation, and by means of committing unthinkable human Rights abuses. Both the Sudanese Central Government and the SPLM/SPLA rewarded those who changed allegiances, pardoning their crimes they committed on the opposing sides, and giving them trust and power to commit more wrong at their conveniences.

During the north-south war, disgruntled SPLA soldiers who committed some sorts of an unacceptable acts run to the Sudanese Armed Forces, and were received with opened hands.

69   Cockett, Richard. Sudan: The Failure and Division of an African State. Yale Press/New Haven and London, 2010.

It became a practice as the war raged, and quite many low-ranking officers left the SPLA under similar circumstances, and made a big gain on the other side of the military showdown. Every conflict has instigators, and every instability has spoilers. It has been observed that various political factions, including the government, armed rebels and even oil companies have committed egregious human rights violations (Maszka, 2019).[70] The war theater had not been a labeled field. The earlier junior officers who left the SPLM/SPLA and made political gain with the Sudanese Government were: Pualino Matip Nhial, Gabriel Gatwech Changson (Tangynyang), Peter Gatdet Yak and many more. The prime examples of monsters who took with them bulk of the SPLA's defectors of 1991: Dr. Riek Machar, Dr. Lam Akol, and Cdr Gordon Kong Chol. In the first two years after the South Sudan's independence, particularly the war of 1991, some Generals who responded to the call by Dr. Riek Machar, and to specifically depose President Salva Kiir Mayardit from power were: Gen. Peter Gatdet Yak who bushered Gen. Ajak Yen as his deputy in SPLA's Division 8 in Panpandiar Military Barrack, overrun the town of Bor, and went into Lou Nuer's Region to recruit young men.

In the eastern Upper Nile, General Gathoth Gatkuoth Hothnyang swiftly responded to the call for toppling the Regime of President Salva Kiir, ransacked villages on his way to town of Malakal, lost the town to the SPLA, recaptured it and

---

70   Maszka, John (2019). A Strategic Analysis of Conflict in Sudan and South Sudan. International Affairs and Global Strategy. https://www.academia.edu/38931570/A_Strategic_Analysis_of_Conflict_in_Sudan_and_South_Sudan

was finally dislodged by air bombardment that raced the town to zero. During the crisis, and during the peace negotiations in Addis Ababa, Ethiopia, General Peter Gatdet and General Gathoth Gatkuoth were opposed to peaceful settlement of the conflict, wanted fight until President Salva Kiir is toppled militarily. That firm stance on military solution did not sit well with Dr. Riek Machar, mounting pressures around the Globe led to Dr. Riek Machar disagreeing with his Chief of General Staff (Peter Gatdet Yak) and his field operations General (Gathoth Gatkuoth Hothnyang). The rhetorics of the two warlords led to them being named in the inquiry on atrocities committed in many parts of the Greater Upper Nile Region of South Sudan.

The two SPLM-IO Generals were let go by Dr. Riek Machar since no one would try to hold on to people who are more likely to be indicted comes the investigation of war crimes and crimes against humanity. At first, the two Generals decided to form their own Rebel Movement (Federal Democratic Party), and led by the solvent politician, Gabriel Chang Changson. But lack of expertise in running a successful guerrilla Movement compelled Gabriel Chang Changson and Gathoth Gatkuoth Hothnyang to agree to amnesty offered by President Salva Kiir's Government, General Gatdet was holed up in Khartoum looking outward. They sought sanctuary under the Government of South Sudan as members of Federal Democratic Party, supposedly led by Gabriel Chang Changson, and where he was appointed Minister for Public Service, and Human Resource Development. By that time, the table has turned rapidly, and General Peter Gatdet's remain dire, but instead to stay in

Khartoum with the old enemy (Al-Bashir of the Sudan).

In all that confusions, and at the time went the Government of South Sudan appeared to have unbeatable strength in the battlefield, General Gathoth Gatkuoth went to Juba as a chair of the Federal Democratic Party's Advance whose they petty peace in with the Government promised them a small share in the Regime, but his own personal interest led to being disowned by his Group in Nairobi, and elsewhere. After the skirmishes of July 8, 2016, and when Riek Machar was on a hot pursuit to DRC, Gathoth Gatkuoth was tactically moved to the SPLM-IO Crown Hotel Dwellers under Taban Deng Gai who assumed the leadership of SPLM-IO, and later became the First vice President for the Republic of South Sudan when all the plans to rid of the SPLM-IO never materialized.

The story never ended there, and SPLA under President Salva Kiir recoiled itself in politics of who should take the blame for the alleged humans right abuses. That time, General Paul Malong Awan, and who saved President Salva Kiir from all the many militias who ganged against the Government met his own demise. The influential nations of the West, especially the United States, the United Kingdoms, and the Kingdoms of Norway wanted the international community wanted sanctioned those behind ruthless killing of civilians across South Sudan. The United States named Paul Malong and others in a targeted sanction. That time around, those close to President Kiir start framing the all times war hero, and he was sacked in May 2017.

In loving memory of Victims of Duk's Massacre on 27th November 2017:

Deng Yuol Ader – Chief (2) Lual Machuk Nhial– Chief (3) Nyandeng Nyakan Malek–Child (4) Jok Mayul Reath– Child (5) Nyuon Chol Nhial. Child (6) Lueth Ket Rabang–Child (7) Akech Atem–Child (8) Deng Leek Deng –Soldier (9) Duot Deng Duot– CRS (10) Diing Deng Monybeer– CRS (11) Ajah Chol Ajack (12) Nyagach Bayak Diu(13) Mayen Mapur Kuai (14) Adut Rou Pajok (15) Maker Anyang Ayom (16) Abul Yhen Bol (17) Kuthin Deng Dut (18) Riak Kuir Koyor (19) Adau Deng Duot (20) Achol Manyik Yai (21) Ajah Malok Deng (22) Abuk Bol Ater (23) Nyandeng Thon Ayuel(24) Ayul Kok Deng (25)Yany Lam (26) Mageu Riak Aleer (27) Chol Nyot Lual (28) Kuai Lul Guet (29) Nyaker Tut Tong (30) Achol Yuol Ader (31) Makuei Atem Goch. Soldier (32) Apiir Machut Ake-ch (33) Nyawai Nuer (34) Achok Manyok Puot (35) Dr. Biar Chagai Biar (36) Aweek Mayek Aleer (37) Juma Pitia John (38) Ajah Mayul Reath (39) Magai Bang Deng (40) Nyamot Kanjai (41) Nyapayuel Mayul (42) a Driver of John Dau Foundation.

The intertribal conflict did not end with Duk incident, it continued across South Sudan, and in areas where Dinkas are the sole residents. In Lakes states (E & W), there report-ed clashes, Agaar-Ruop and Agaar-Pakaam were caught up in fighting which started on December 6, 2017, and by December 8, 2017, confirmed reports placed death tolls at 115. The first fighting recorded a death of 70 people, and on Friday, there

S/No	Names in Full	Sex	Age	Abducted R.
1	Achot Mayul Reeth	16	F	
2	Aduk Mayul Reath	6	F	
3	Chol Riek Deng	11	M	
4	Bol Hoth Thet	11	M	
5	Alek Panther Ruot	4M	F	
6	Abul Makoi Kithou	10	F	
7	Atuong Nyankiir Maduk	12	F	
8	Ayen Lual Machok	4	F	
9	Nyakong Ruach Weituo	10	F	
10	Nyanyuot Ruach Weituor	8	F	
11	Nyacouty Ruach Weituor	6	F	
12	Aker Deng Manyuon	12	"	
13	Adol Deng Manyuon	8	"	
14	Agot Deng Manyuon	5	"	
15	Nyanduk Kuei Lul	7	"	
16	Makim Kuei Lul	10	M	
17	Kuei Kong Awual	45	F	
18	Machuei Ruot Rou	10	M	
19	Lual Ruot Rou	8	M	
20	Nyaliep Ruot Rou	4	F	
21	Nyibol Ruot Rou	4	"	
22	Majok Pakok Manguak	14	M	
23	Lul Thou Lul	7	M	
24	Chongkuach Majok Awan	2	M	
25	Akei Koryom Ajiing	7	F	
26	Ajok Koryom Ajiing	4	F	
27	Manyiel Bol Kuen	3	M	
28	Nyamuot Kong Gach	15	F	
29	Tap Kong Gach	11	M	
30	Magot Chol Nyot	11	"	
31	Lual Abiel Lul	4	M	
32	Agot Deng Manyiel	5	F	
33	Akur Deng Manyiel	5	F	
34	Bol Deng Manyiel	8	M	
35	Awan Deng Manyiel	1	M	

	No	Name	Age	Sex
	36	Akur Deng Riak	7	F
	37	Kuei Deng Riak	4	"
	38	Loch Deng Riak	3	M
	39	Tar Deng Riak	1	F
	40	Yai Deng Riak	1	M
	41	Deng Maker Ayong	5	M
	42	Bol Chol Bol	7	M
	43	Adhk Chol Bol	5	F
	44	Akech Machot Akech	8	M
	45	Aluel Kon Nyok	6	F
	46	Arjen Chol Ayual	7	F
	47	Ayual Chol Ayual	5	M
	48	Arjenthii Chol Ayual	1	F
	49	Nyandom Chol Ayual	3	F
	50	Maduk Mapur Kuai	5	M
	51	Mawut Lam Jok	11	M
	52	Nyaluak Lam Jok	6	F
	53	Taban Lam Jok	8	M
	54	Borchay Lam Jok	12	M
	55	Bol Njibol Mawut Makuei	4	F
	56	Achol Kuei Lul	12	F

The copy of the hand written names was sent by Ayuel Aleer Deng Malual. The list was sent by AyuelAleer as mentioned above, a relative who was in close contact with those involved in rescue and transport of the wounded to Juba. The Nyarweng youths in Diaspora did exceptionally well, responded rapidly and chartered a Red Cross plane to airlift the wounded from Duk directly to Juba where they were treated for guns shots. It was a terrible moment, and people in South Sudan and around the world were shocked by the heinous crime committed onto the civil population.

were another 45 killed in revenge attack. The surge of violence seemed to be end of the year thing in South Sudan, and the Government was not in a position to contain fighting given the ongoing war in the country. In the same region, there was also an intercommunal fighting in Aliab Dinka areas that resulted into death of four people.

In all of that, South Sudanese were left with prayers only, the authorities, being crippled by the civil war in the country had no compacity to break up, not even a small fight in the countryside. The cattle rearing communities in South Sudan have proven themselves to be addicted to violence, and their armed races contributed to instability in the country; increased number of displaced person, and exacerbated a humanitarian crisis. It was a wishful thinking of the northern Sudanese during the 50-years liberation struggle in South that the people of Southern Sudan would not be able to govern themselves effectively given their intolerance, and prenninal fighting among themselves.

Despite the rhetoric being a direct incitement, the charge have some truth to it because some high-ranking individuals in South Sudan have been involved in communal feuds, some supplied ammunitions to their communities, and all were used to lynch the opposing side. If anything, then it is lack of political maturity that led such individuals not to rise above local neighhood politics. For some, supplying firearms to the local youth was a patriotic duty to the community, and they garnished lots of praises from tribal chiefs whose interest is to continue to be relevant in the face of changing world. With technology being available almost everywhere, the youth who go on raiding mission connect with their supporters via satellite telephone, and give information as how they are doing in the battlefields. The other side of the same coin is, how can land with such activities be made productive? There is zero chance that investors would attempt to set up farms in an environment where youths constantly butcher themselves, and no law to curtail their acts. South Sudan as a whole is embroiled in inter-enthnic conflicts, often involves cattle-rustling and rivalry over control of land and pastures.

Golden years of Gen. Paul Malong Awan

When the SPLM/SPLA's founder, Dr. John Garang de Mabior was no more, a lot of changes occurred within the files and ranks of the SPLA. Those changes reflected a new dawn in what later became the Republic of South Sudan. One of critical assignment was given to General Malong, and as the commander

Gen. Paul Malong as SPLA's Chief of General Staff_Bilpam file photo

of Presidential Guards(Tiger Battalion). Like any other head of such Unit around the world, General Paul Malong was tasked with the personal security Commander in chief of the SPLA and the First vice President of the Republic of Sudan, the work that Gen. Malong would do exceptionally well. Having earned the respect of the President of Southern Sudan, Gen. Malong was appointed as a Governor of Northern Bahr El Ghazal.

During his tenure as a Governor, Malong was very active in the Region's politics, and stood shoulder to shoulder with President Salva Kiir. Shortly before the SPLM political showdown in 2013, Governor Malong organized the Bahr El Ghazal

Region's Governors conference, which was held in the town of Wau, Western Bahr El Ghazal state. The overall objective of the Governors' conference was to show solidarity with President Salva Kiir, give him all the supports necessary to let him hold on to power as President of Republic of South Sudan. In that meeting, Governor Malong called people out, particularly Madam Nyandeng Malek, the then Governor of Warrap states, and where the president hails from. Governor Malong pointed out that Governor Nyandeng Malek should have been leading in support of the president because she is Governor of the President's home state.

Since that time, a lot of things went wrong, and the biggest being the starting of war on December 15, 2013. Given previous interests shown by Governor Malong, he was reinstated in the national Army, promoted from rank of Major General to the rank of 1st Lt. General and made the Army Chief of the General Staff. As a renowned fighter, Malong successfully fought against Rebels of Dr. Riek Machar and other splinter Groups who wanted to rid of President Salva Kiir Mayardit. Threes down the road, the war turned out to be disastrous, and all the attempts by the Regional and the International community to resolve the conflict were given consideration. The chairman and commander in chief of the SPLM-IO, Dr. Riek Machar returned to Juba.

In just three months since his returned, a conflict erupted, this time near Presidential Palace(J1). The cloudy politics of the senseless conflict let to Dr. Riek Machar of the SPLM-IO being dislodged from Juba, chased for 37 days toward the

General Paul Malong(L) with President Salva Kiir (R)

*Statue of Dr. Garangduring Independence Day
(July 9, 2011)-File Photo.*

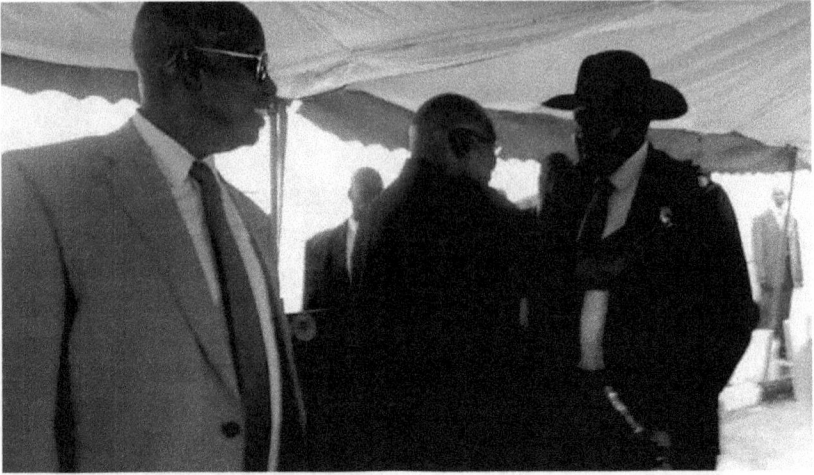

Dr. Francis Mading Deng (L), Gen. Paul Malong (C)
& President Kiir (R).

Democratic Republic of the Congo (DRC), and extracted from the Democratic Republic of the Congo (DRC) to Khartoum, Sudan, and later to Ethiopia. Thereafter, Dr. Riek Machar went to South Africa, and allegedly detained by the South African authorities on the recommendation of the Government of South Sudan, Regional Bloc(IGAD), and the Troika (Kingdoms of Norway, United States of America and the United Kingdom). The designated post of the First Vice President of the Transitional Government of National Unity(TGoNU) was later given Taban Deng Gai, formerly Chief Negotiator on behalf of the SPLM-IO, and one of the three charged and convicted in absentia for attempted coup after the night of December 15, 2013.

"The war mongers in this country had hoped the recent crisis would explode. They were talking, and I was getting all that they were saying but I decided to pursue peaceful means because General Malong is a hero who contributed to the history of this country, and I did not want to see what happened to the leaders like Cdr. KerubinoKuanyinBol and Cdr. William NyuonBany, who contributed to the history of South Sudan happens again. Kerubino and William Nyuon contributed but their end was unhappy, and this is what we do not want to repeat this time with my comrade Paul Malong"[71], Pres. Salva Kiir during the reconciliation with Paul Malong.

Conditions for Peace

Riek Machar can come back to Juba here, but without even a single soldier. If they say he will return with his army, I will never accept," Kiir said at a ceremony of the army flag handover to the new army chief in Juba on Thursday. "I told them that you people [regional leaders] Riek Machar is a South Sudanese citizen. As government of South Sudan, we have not cancelled Machar's citizenship. So I told them to bring Riek Machar," he said. "I said you bring Riek Machar to Juba here. Bring him to Juba and I will guarantee his safety, and I will protect him with the national army. If you don't believe me, the RPF is here. You bring the RPF to take charge of the security of Riek Machar in

---

71   http://www.sudantribune.com/spip.php?article64028

SALVA KIIR
PRESIDENT, SOUTH SUDAN

*President attending news Conference
on December 15, 2013._Gurtong.net*

Juba," Kiir said in a recorded audio obtained by Radio Tama-zuj.[72]

On totality of what would really means a truly liberated country, there remains a lot of work to be done. It appeared that former guerrilla commanders have not learned much from their two decades in the bush, and eleven years running their own affairs. Instead of transitioning into Statehood, and planting a more just society, the SPLA's Generals, and as they like to be referred to still live a bushlife in liberated land, and citizens lived more like there is another tomorrow left for them. Over the

---

72   The prospect for peace has not been a priority to people within the circle of President Salva Kiir. He kept setting conditions contrary to citizens' expectation. Pres. Salva Kiir's comment quoted above carried a thick message, peace not being a priority to him. https://radiotamazuj.org/en/news/article/kiir-sets-1-condition-for-machar-s-return-to south-sudan

years, wars have been waged in the territories of SUDAN and many unsuccessful peace accords have been initiated. The major peace accords were the Addiss Ababa Peace Agreement(1972) and the Comprehensive Peace Agreement(2005).

The noticeable differences between the Addis Ababa Peace Agreement (1972) and the Comprehensive Peace Agreement(2005) are: (a). The Southern Sudan Rebels retained their military wing, the SPLA, (b). Autnomous Government with specific mandare was established in Southern Sudan, (c). The right to Self-Determination with option to conduct a Referendum on the future of Southern Sudan was guaranteed by the CPA, (d). The main Source of income (Oil) was penned down to be split 50-50.

A few small lessons have learned. Seventy-nine years after Tamburabetrayal, his grandson, Joseph James Tambura, then the head of the Southern Regional Government, betrayed the trust given him by his people when he and others conspired with authorities of the central government in 1983 to abrogate the Addis Ababa Agreement, in exchange for making him the nominal governor of Equatoria.[73] Page 16, para. 4.

The setback seens over the past decades came from South Sudanese and South Sudanese themselves. Without a unified fronts, whether in development or building strong econom-ic, politican and social instituions, not much can materialize. South Sudanese are well known for creating best job titles for Government's employees, servicing officials to the max and

73   Alier, Abel. Southern Sudan: Too Many Agreements Dishonoured. New York: Ithaca Press, 1990.

paying no attention to the purpose of Government's institutions. The freedom that South Sudanese yarned for more than five decades is either few decades away or not yet complete. It would make no sense for a land to be liberated from the oppressors, and then the liberated still linger all over the world, hundreds of thousands in internally displaced campsshortly after the country's independence.

Anything contrary to the liberation principles is just an insult to the martyrs who made the ultimate sacrifices for the people of South Sudan. The much-celebrated process in the recent years has been the subdivision of South Sudan in many states. One would expect a popular demand by the people to deliver what it was meant for. Since the independence of the Republic of South Sudan, few significant celebrations have been seen, but the case of federal states have illuminated the airwaves.

Most people in the rural areas and some in urban areas immediatelt felt the anxiety of the economic consequences of war, as the civilains population has always found itself caught at the crossroads in such situations of the sudden outbreak of violence.[74]

After they wasted too much money and presided over war that killed thousands of innocent civilians, South Sudanese leaders, and under the auspices of President Salva Kiir resorted to dividing the country into smaller units, just to buy time such that their reigning over the helpless is not stopped. What the current leaders called "popular demand by the people" may be

---

74   Jok, Madut Jok. Sudan: Race, Religion, And Violence. Oneworld Publications. Oxford, 2007.

a different call or misinterpretation of Dr. John Garang's town to people. Some people like to refer to as SPLM's vision, forgetting that SPLM collapsed after John Garang was no more. How possible is it that redistricting is done in the middle of a civil war. Records showed that further subdivision of the country into smaller administrative units, some called it ethnic federal states came after South Sudan inflicted a deep wound onto itself, the citizens bought into the new idea of bushes into states, a reincarnation of the SPLM's vision of taking town to people. It would not hurt to call call it an ecstasy of political maneuvering as the base hold no glue whatsoever.

CHAPTER THREE

South Sudan's political turbulence is akin to the chaotic structure of a stream of water from a tap:unpredictable from moment to moment, but retaining its basic structure over time. South Sudan became this way primarily because of how Sudan governed its peripheries with a system of monetized and militarized tribalism.[75]

Democracy in South Sudan

For many generations, political activists in South South campaigned vigorously for democratic governance, and have used their vivid understanding of the system to wage a successful fight against Kharotum. The proclamation fitted perfectly with

---

75   De Waal, A. (2014). When kleptocracy becomes insolvent: brute causes of the civil war in South Sudan. African Affairs, (452), 347.

quest for independent South Sudan, which citizens voted almost unaminously in the 2011 Referendum has not been fulfilled. The world's newest State fell into traps: vicious cycles of tribal based conflicts, institutionalized corruption, and political unrests. One of the contributing factors to South Sudan's post-independence crisis was the government's failure to use the six-year interim period before the independence referendum to confront directly the internal wounds of the civil war and promote reconciliation between South Sudanese communities (Johnson, 2016, p. 176). South Sudanese need a better framework to be able to appreciate the importance of founding principles.

The Interim Constitution of South Sudan is the legal basis that set the foundation for governance, and as dictated by many Articles of that made of the Governing Document. What remained as a myth is how South Sudan would utilize the system they longed for many decades, and the sacrifices to attain the independence of South Sudan. South Sudanese intellectuals must condemn and oppose the use of violence in resolving the crises of governance and leadership facing the country (Deng, 2020, p. 69). The South Sudanese scholars from all walks of life have missed call the intellectuals move the national agenda.

Having diversity in papers alone cannot make the country livable and sustainable in the face of many globalized crises. It is a bitter truth that tribes in South Sudan live more like foreigners, single national identity has not been forged, no enough glue that holds the many nations (tribal terrories) together. The old Sudan had done absolutely nothing to unify the now people of the Republic of South Sudan. The old concept was that Southerners deserve nothing. The tyrants who ruled the Sudan had one thing in common; they used ethnic and subethnic divisions to make political gains for themselves.

Ethnic conflict in Africa has been viewed as a product of tyranny; it has been and continued to be a tactic that tyrants use to divide and rule.[76] With the experience from all the conflicts in the Sudan and the South Sudan, leaders should have done a great deal to bring the enthnicities together, shape their future, and create an atmosphere where citizens see themselves as one people. The people of South Sudan were made to fight senseless wars among themselves, militias were created to advance interest of the Sudanese central government, anominosity coined up, and stereotypes drummed to the point where tribes hated themselves to hell.

As fragile as the nation of South Sudan is, those who are ambitious to lead the country must do extra works, get deep into the villages, and try to change the mindsets of the majority who have never seen a government before. Assumption has it that people would be in compliance with the rule of law, and the social order that can sustain a working economy. That behavior of citizens know it all does not holds any truth to it, and englightened people should have known better than the layperson in the villaged. Without a meaningful education, even a small disagreements often unthinkable conflicts.

---

76   Berkeley, Bill. (2001). Race, Tribe, and Power in the Heart of Africa. World Policy Journal, 18(1), 79. https://search-ebscohost-com.lopes.idm.oclc.org/login.aspx?direct=true&db=edsjsr&AN=edsjsr.40209734&site=eds-live&scope=site

The way in which a country is governed in terms of accommodating differences among its components determines whether their leaders would build or dismantle their nation.[77]

The country called the Republic of South Sudan is tribally polarized, and democracy does not follow the logic of differing political opinion. Quite often, people converged and diversged, the alliances do not stick together as stakeholders choose to go with their tribemen or those who remain behind are eliminated by all possible means. When the SPLM/SPLA formed in 1983, there were those who favored a secessionist agenda and those who want a reformists agenda for the people of SUDAN. Because the two political positions represented two kinds of people who wanted a liberation of Sudanese, but through different means. It had happened majority of those who refused to join the Addis Ababa Agreeement in 1972 wanted an independent South Sudan while who rebelled in height of Islamization by President Jafaar Mohamed Nimeiri who wanted to reformthe Sudan's political system, and by installing secular State. In every fight, ethnicity pay great roles in South Sudanese politics, and it surely played crucial role in the SPLM/SPLA's split in 1983, and again in 1991.

Regardless of his leadership struggle with Dr. Garang, Akuot Atem de Mayen was just executed as a Dinka, believed to have been planted by Garang in order to wreck the Nuer's Movement from within. William Abdalla Chuol, who assumed power upon the death of Akuot Atem, changed the the name of

---

77   Nasredeen, A. (2013). Identities and citizenship in Sudan: Governing constitutional principles. African Human Rights Law Journal, (2), 383.

his Movement from SPLM/SPLA to Anya-Nya II.[78]

Subdivision of South Sudan Into Ethnic States

Ethnicity appears to have acquired an ever-denser tangibility in South Sudanese politics, for a number of reasons. First, economic development has taken place in territories historically divided among different ethnic groups, and partially administered by traditional authorities drawn from those groups- and that economic development happened unevenly. It created spatial hierarchies often promote or demote people according to ethnicity. Secondly, rural government systems emphasized ethnicity, drawing administrative borders around sectional and sub-sectional territories. Thirdly, these territories and the sections that inhabit them are the constituencies for South Sudan's politicians, who were often unable to manage political base through resource allocation, and have been tempted into Mobilizing them by invoking fears of 'ethnic demotion' instead.[79]

Peace is not necessary the absence of violence, but a combination of all things that make countries flourish. The tensions among various ethnic groups in South Sudan, and the tribal

---

78   Arop, Madut-Arop. Sudan's Painful Road to Peace. A Full Story of The Founding and Development of the SPLM/SPLA. BookSurge, LLC., 2006. The first chairman of the SPLM/SPLA was slain by his subordinates for being a Dinka, and suspected to be working for Dinka's political agenda. It that kind of mistrust that ignite most ethnic conflict in South Sudan.

79   Thomas, (2015, p.160). South Sudan: A Slow Liberation. Observors agreed that South Sudan is too polarized; jobs and constitutional posts are allocated based on ethnicity. This among others is responsible for the subdivision of the country into smaller states.

animosity tells the other side of the unknown story. All indications make it dubious for anyone with conscience mind to accept a better result from the sprinklers of the infant State. The nation of South Sudan slipped and tripped so badly that a surrounding wall was subjected to grievous injuries of the higher order. One would assumed that all lives and properties are under the sole protection of the State, and freedom of association is guaranteed as prescribed by the Interim Constitution, and other traditional principles that protects interests of the people within defined territory of South Sudan. It's on this template that a license to author a short term tour of other countries where people's interests are protected.

The devolution of power reduces the dominance of another ethnic group at the intergroup level without creating new dominance within the realm of the self-government arrangement: no single subgroup must fear domination and repression by another subgroup. Thus, it is hardly promising for elites to try to mobilize support based on exclusionary ethnic agendas that emphasize threats emanating from other subgroups.[80]

When states were proliferated, first echoed by the then Rebels' leader, Dr. Riek Machar of the Sudan People's Liberation Movement in Opposition (SPLM-IO), and who based his call for ethnic federalism with the pretext of 21 former British District in Southern Sudan. The decision by the SPLM-IO

---

80   De Juan, A. (2013). Devolving Ethnic Conflicts: The Role of Subgroup Identities for Institutional Intergroup Settlements. Civil Wars, 15(1), 78. doi:10.108 0/13698249.2013.781304. https://lopes.idm.oclc.org/login?url=http://search.ebscohost.com/login.aspx?direct=true&db=edb&AN=87373928&site=eds-live&scope=site

as it appeared to be very popular that time was picked up by the most powerful Jieng Council of Elders (JCE), sold to the President of South Sudan, and cemented by interest to stay in power indefinitely. The whole skirmish turned out to be an opening of a political pandora box, and every village wanted a state of its own. The Governors of the newly established federal states bypassed the president, and started acting far more than their Boss (the President of the Republic). Throughout South Sudan, though states were dysfunctional, the newly handpicked Governors maneuvered with their local governments, appointing and sacking counties commissioners.

The state of comic was alleviated to the next level, and all the political analysts are left speechless. A different front was opened among various subtribes, and that clearly showed the well calculated "divide and rule" strategy by the ruling Elites who saw Presidnet Salva Kiir as one of their own, and has to be kept in power indefinitely. While war raged between the Sudan People's Liberation Movement/Army-in-Opposition and the Government of South Sudan, some splinter groups fought parally, and against the Government. Most of those who were disgruntled Army Generals from ethnic minorities in the Greater Equatoria took up arms against the Government and used their tribal bases to wage the war. The two who broke ties with the Government of South Sudan were: Gen. Thomas Cirillo Swaka, the then Deputy Chief of the SPLA General Staff, and Joseph Bakasoro, the only independent candidate who won gubernatorial race in 2010, and became Governor of the Western Equatoria state.

At some points during the 2013-2016 conflict, Governor

Joseph Bakasoro of the Western Equatoria state was placed under arrest shortly after being removed from governorship. When he was released, Bakasoro went on and started his negative campaign against the Government, called it a tribal Regime. It was not too long before General Thomas Cirillo quitted his position as the SPLA's deputy Chief of General Staff. While a new Rebel commander-in-chief, Swaka released number of position papers, and was interviewed by major news agencies in East Africa. A crucial interview was made by Chris Kiwawulo of the New Vision Newspaper(Uganda) posed a series of question of questions to Thomas Cirillo Swaka as a former Deputy Chief of General Staff of the South Sudan national Army (SPLA), but the selected question specifically asked a tribal question, and tribal answers were given by Gen. Cirillo of the National Salvation Army.

You say Kiir has turned SPLA into a partisan and tribal army, why didn't you simply advise him against that, so he could change instead of resigning? We have been advising Kiir as one of the comrades and our leaders during the start of SPLA. We have been advising him after the peace agreement was signed, but he rubbished us. Kiir started establishing tribal groups in the army. We were talking to him for the security of our people. But I think Kiir and his tribal group have plans to control the country. Throughout this time, we have been talking to him, and the defense council used to sit and discuss the issue of forming a national army. But Kiir and his group were not interested in sharing the command of the national army. My decision to quit the government and form the National Salvation Front (NSF) was a result of Kiir failing to listen to anybody. He refused all our advice to form a national army. The glory of SPLA is no longer there. It is now a bigger militia.[81]

For many decades since British left Sudan, there have been conversations in the South, most of which talked about forging unity in diversity. As South Sudanese tried to move away from tribal mindsets, elites and sociopolitical activists have struggling with defining a new society where ethnicity does not prevent people from meeting their political aspirations. The many wars in the South, majority against the north, and tribes against tribes have hurdled off conducive environment for political maturity. There were many attempts by the Southern's political elites to create South Sudan through self-rule, and Addis Ababa Agreement. The peace, however, created a limited autonomous region that was more likely to be rammed by the grantor. Within that Peace Accord were political loopholes that gave the Sudanese central Government crude excuse, and reason to dismantle the Agreement in its entireity, and returned the Region (Southern Sudan) under Khartuom's rule. The struggle against the Sudanese governments was aided by lack of trust among the Southern Sudanese, and where ethnicity played the "divide and conquer" roles.

The removal of Abel Alier as the chief executie of the South with active participation of many Dinka politicians and his replacement by the former Anya Nya leader General Joseph Lagu who hails from minority Madi people was seen by many

81   Kiwawulo, Chris. (2017). https://www.newvision.co.ug/new_vision/news/1455746/gen-swaka-explains-source-sudan-conflict-appeals-museveni

observers as a proof that the people of Southern Sudan had risen above narrow ethnic politics. Critics, however, took the contrary view, arguing that the Dinka leaders who helped bring Lagu to power simply wanted to use him while pretending to be liberal; in other words, eating and having the cake at the same time.[82]

Copy-Paste of Divide and Misrule from the Old Sudan

The government of South Sudan began to resemble those aspects of the Khartoum regime, SPLM repeatedly repudiated: the concentration of power in the power of the president; interference in the administration of the states by the central government, and impunity of an increasingly arbitrary state security service (Johnson, 2016, p.175). The South Sudanese have not been that independent from the host country of Sudan. In years following Sudan's independence, Sudanese governments played tribal political cards, and by setting tribes against themselves. Even in the quest for independent South Sudan, ethnic divisions were used to frustrate the cause for the people of South Sudan, and create a power struggle that stretched the rulers of northerners over southerners for five decades. The strategy was straightforward, exploit the illiterate masses, and empower the few who saw political power as avenue for wealth and personal pride.

Nimeiri took advantage of the rift which existed between the

82   Atem, Atem Yaak. Jungle Chronicles and Other Writings: Recollections of A South Sudanese. Africa World books, 2017.

Dinka leadership and the leaders of the smaller tribes, especially General Lagu, who came out strongly in favor of the division of the Southern Sudan region, hoping to get a better deal fro himself inside Equatoria........He was not championing the cause of the smaller tribes in the face of Dinka domination; he was simply dividing to misrule.[83]

When the South seceded from South, freedom-fighters copied and pasted what they once called as margrnization and misrule of the Africans in the Sudan. In many cases, the things that politicians do in South Sudan are replicas of what politicians have done in the Sudan (north). For example, arbitrary detention of journalists, the surge of extrajudicial killing in South Sudan's towns, and polarization of ethnic differences are all political trations in the Sudan, and have been imported into newest State. What troubled observors is how South Sudan is setting itself out of the bad system of govenance it had left behind? Of course, cultural similarities do existed, but the platform upon which Sudanese played was not all uniform; Southern Sudanese were less of citizens in the Sudan, and anything of the kind should not be practiced in South Sudan under any circumstance.

The people of South Sudan have made a name for themselves, and by speaking against injustice, human rights abuses and political margnization. For such to hold substances, people must shift away from tribal politics, regional affiliation mindset ought to be discarded altogether, and make a country to

83   Khalid, Mansour. Nimeiri and the Revolution of Dis-may. London: Kegan Paul, 1985.

accommodate its citizens regardless of ethnic identity. The political atmosphere in the country has not worked well for all the citizens, fakes political alliances have been sprearheaded by the elites.

Buying into Historical Grudges

The South-South violence that escalated during the 1990s as the SPLA battled its Southern opponents by targeting civilian communities, and vice versa, produced absolutist perceptions still viscerally present. During that time, the SPLA perceived its militia opponents and the subsequent retribution raids against their home communities as a 'national security issue' that must be brutally dealt with to protect the revolution, whereas the anti-SPLA opposition saw its own violence against Southern Communities as 'countering Dinka domination (LeRiche, & Arnold, 2013, p. 230).

In some parts of Africa, the newer forms of rustling have increased the sheer numbers of livestock stolen, and concomitantly the raids have resulted in an almost exponential increase in violence (Cline, 2020). South Sudanese have never lived without crises, violence has always part of the South Sudanese. As cattle-rearing society, people have fought over pastures and water sources. This has been dealt with by the colonial powers, the Sudanese succesive regimes, and the autonomous governments that have ever existed in South Sudan prior to independence. What was unique about the previously documented conflicts was the scale of damage. The tribal war fought were mostly fought using traditonal weapons; spears, rods and axes. With introduced of automated weapons, the cost of those fights skyrocked, too many people killed in just matter of hours, large herds of animals looted, villages burned down and thousands displaced. The trend need a modern approach, a strong government that is able to arrest the situation, and control ruthless activities by the South Sudanese traditional societies.

On The Western Democracy

The concept called democracy started in some lands far away from Africa, was imported into the continent of Africa and elsewhere in the world. The United States adopted the democratic govenance, enshrone its into their constitution, and become the law of the land. In all level of power distribution, aspiring leaders run for offices, get elected and takes on the service as prescribed in the constitution. In one of the historic election in the modern American history, something so foreign to the Americans took place in Washington DC as masses rioted their way into the Capitol in protest against the election's resultion. Reacting to riot on Capitol Hill on January 6, 2021, Former US President, George Walker Bush had this to say:

"Laura and I are watching the scenes of mayhem unfolding at the seat of our Nation's government in disbelief and dismay. It is a sickening and heartbreaking sight. This is how election results are disputed in a banana republic – not our democratic republic. I am appalled by the reckless behavior of some political leaders since the election and by the lack of respect shown today for our institutions, our traditions, and our law enforcement."[84]

Well, democracy around the world is not the same, but fundamentals of the so-called DEMOCRACY are the same. When election are conducted, the outcomes must be respected, those who lost elections are supposed to vacate their posts in peace, respect the rule of law, uphold the constitution, and leave no stain of hatred behind. Whenever there is a misstep somewhere in system, the country who have only taken the cover of democracy are not missed. The term "banana republic" pretty much refers to developing nations, mostly in Latin America and Africa. Most leaders in those countries have taken democracy as way to climb the political ladder, stay in power while using the cover, and not practice anything about democracy.

It's well noted that, known dictators of the world present themselves as democrats, as they do the exact opposite. For example, col. Gadaffi of Libya was known within his own country as a democratic leader despite how he rose to power and single handedly run the country. In a long list of dictators; Saddam Huisen of Iraq was the brutal dictator; Hosni Mubarak of Egypt was a down to Earth dictator, Fidel Castro of Cuba, Hugo Chavez of Venezuela was another other. In other scenario, Samuel Doe and Charles Taylor of Liberia were abstractly Democrats so was Meles Zenawi of Ethiopia, Aferwaki of Eritrea, Robert Mugabe of Zimbabwe, Paul Kageme of Rwanda,

---

84   'It's A Sickening, Heartbreaking Sight': Former President George W. Bush Reacts To Chaos At US Capitol. CBSDFW.com Staff January 6, 2021 at 5:24 pm. https://dfw.cbslocal.com/2021/01/06/sickening-heartbreaking-former-president-george-w-bush-chaos-capitol/

Yoweri Museveni of Uganda, Omari Al-Bashir of Sudan and Salva Kiir of South Sudan.

CHAPTER FOUR

Politial Power in South Sudan

Most of the power in South Sudan is held by the military; in that military, those with political power, namely Salva Kiir and Riek Machar, have an ethnically charged atmosphere that integrates ethnic tribalism with politics, allowing citizens and political organizations to base support for a leader on his tribal affiliation.[85]

In a nutshill, presumed political solutions never lasts in a practical senses. As society transform, new political forces and poltical ideological develp, and political landscape change with new demands and challenges. The political setup of the State of South Sudan appears to incompatible with structures

---

85   Omer, R. (2016). South Sudan: from independence to a detrimental civil war. Harvard International Review, (3), 11.

of modern States. All things considered, the people of South Sudan were prepared to secede from rest of the Sudan, but did not enough capacity to build a prosperous State in Africa. One of the biggest challenges that continue haunt South Sudanese is separating personal ambition for political power and community's interest. Those individuals who want to rise to the top use all possible means to achieve their desires.

In much of South Sudan's rural areas, there is force in the waiting. Communal militias may align with parties to the civil war but may not be fully controlled by either the government or rebel groups (Krause, 2019).[86] This has been the case throughout the history of Sudan, South Sudan, and many other African States. Whenever political disagreement goes wild, militias associated with certain ethnic groups pick side, and fight war a way for them to settle their old scores. In 1991 when the SPLA breakaway group under Dr. Riek Machar and Dr. Lam Akol declared the war on the SPLA under Dr. John Garang, remnants of the Anyanya-II joined Riek Machar's faction and torched Dinka's villages in Jonglei province and Upper Nile province. In 2013, militias joined the war and fought on both sides of the conflict.

The last time I witnessed a short cut social discourse was in the 1998 when nonparties to the problem attempted to shovel the earth away. Well, all the participants on this avenue were

---

86   Krause, J. (2019). Stabilization and Local Conflicts: Communal and Civil War in South Sudan. Ethnopolitics, 18(5), 478–493. https://lopes.idm. oclc.org/login?url=https://search.ebscohost.com/login.aspx?direct=true&db=ed-b&AN=137989022&site=eds-live&scope=site&custid=s8333196&groupid=-main&profile=eds1

there, and that should have been a learning experience. For the record, the complexity of the issues involved make it hard for an overnight solution. It's no single person problem, but a deeply rooted issue that require honest political engagement. Picking wrong methods, and selecting wrong venues just widen the problem. There is no doubt, many people in the country were caught off guard, and that is the beauty of having populace in a grey area. It would have died down in few moons, but Mother Nature had the last say to recalibrate.

As governments at war with their citizens become increasingly unable to sustain and control their armies, they turn to local sources of provisioning through counter-insurgency warfare that involves intense predatory behavior of soldiers and their militias.[87]

After four years of military unrests, some conmen took economics opportunities at their disposal, turned into being pro-government overnight, and now there is a different war being waged in the country. The known war was about reforms in all sectors, but so much has changed in the Republic of South Sudan. The war over personalities and economics interest has swiftly titled the political table, and made Rebels at bays.

---

87   Deng, L. B. (2010). Social capital and civil war: The Dinka communities in Sudan's civil war. African Affairs, 109(435), 231-250. https://lopes.idm.oclc.org/login?url=http://search.ebscohost.com/login.aspx?direct=true&db=a9h&AN=51492460&site=eds-live&scope=site

CHAPTER FIVE

Missed Reform Opportunities

A war through reforms and adherence to rule of law is a war worth fighting. For quite sometimes, at least in the critical 7 years of political turmoil (2014-2021), South Sudanese civil society organizations have been more of puppets to the Government. That is nothing, but a loss of a major Battle. In a participatory democracy like South Sudan(in theory), there is an obligation that governments should be open, share what they do openly, publish documents pertaining to their practices and keep citizens informed about new development initiaitives.

Throughout the world, not just South Sudan, civil society organizations work hard to ensure that governments don't overstep their authorities, make sure that illegal activities are don't condoned, make sure that political leaders don't escape justice and make sure that people in government conform to existing laws. Pressure politicians to conform to democratic principles, mobilize, encourage and train future ethical leaders, challenge unwarranted abuse of power by the law enforcement, and arbitrary detention of citizens without due process.

The lack of genuine national agenda from the onset placed everyone in a very bad position to argue against the shortcomings. There has not been a legitimate government has ever since, during the autonomous Government period, after the independence, and so forth. For the worse, the Region once know as Southern Sudan was dubbed into Khartoum's nurtured policies, and started to operate under a police State operated in the Regions that now are South Sudan, and no universal legal frameworks that has ever been adopted by the people of South Sudan apart from their almost unanimous voting for the independence of South Sudan.

South Sudan as a country was born out of curiosity, and through the visions of few who are now no more. The duties and responsibilities of supposedly public officials are not clearly defined or citizens don't see their leaders' limits. When a country is in such situation, civil society organizations need to step up and start offering some information, and how every citizens should treated, how governments (central & states) ought to deal with citizens in their respective jurisdictions. It's a human nature, once a person is in power, he/she doesn't look outside, see no reason to be so restricted, and civil organizations can be proactive, and make sure that nothing is done out of the ordinary. Power struggle in South Sudan dated back to the first

Sudanese civil war, and the second Sudanese civil ware where many Southern Rebels split along ethnic lines.

During the 1990s and 2000s ethnicity became a military strategy for consolidating political power among rebel commanders.[88]

There is a good reason for anyone to be very concern about the way things work in South Sudan. The nation started on a wrong footing, people live more like visitors, having no objectives, short or long terms for the country. This look more like the centuries when Turks and Arabs arrived in the SUDAN, found no political organizations in place, settled the land and start making indigenous do things their way. The people of South Sudan need to arise above in activity, catch-up with the Region and the world within their reach. With the help of the civil organizations, citizens can be invigorated to take charge of their country, start working in labor and social clubs, and own the history of the country. No dead liberator or the minds behind the independence of South Sudan will back to remind the living for what they need to do. Time is about right for informed citizens to shape political processes, and by appreciating the kind of system that they have chosen. There is no single system of government that is better other, but the kind that people have approved, developed and take pride of it.

More than anything else, there has been lack of consistent

88   Kane, R. (2014). Ritual Formation of Peaceful Publics: Sacrifice and Syncretism in South Sudan (1991-2005). Journal of Religion In Africa, 44(3/4), 386-410. https://lopes.idm.oclc.org/login?url=http://search.ebscohost.com/login.aspx?direct=true&db=rlh&AN=101835017&site=eds-live&scope=site

leadership in South Sudan, particularly the way top officials conducted themselves in issues that are crucial to the soeverignty of the state. In many occasion, leaders have been tempted to say things that they should not be saying, acting out of the ordinary, and behaving as heads of households. A country need bold decisions, and positions that reflect muscles of the nation. When South Sudanese President is faced with tough choices, he often lowered his tone to the point of compromising the position he holds as head of the State. Of the many controversial statements by the President, one caused an outraged from the general public:

The fact that South Sudan broke away from Sudan was not really the most choice of everybody, but the majority when they decide in a democratic situation, people have to go with this.[89]

The Cooperation Agreement (2012) between the Republic of South Sudan and the Republic of Sudan created lots of mistrusts, and have caused some people lives and their stay in South Sudan. The Oil transit fee and disputed areas have been mishandled by the Government of the Republic of South Sudan, and public opinion was not given due consideration. Instead of negotiating as equal partners, officials who negotiated on behalf of the people of South Sudan signed agreement that gave away much of the resources as well as leverage over the disputed areas. The Sudanese Government in Khartuom acted as if South Sudan was still under it total control, and South Sudanese on

---

89   President Salva Kiir said on November 1, 2017, while in session with President Omar Al Bashir of the Sudan. http://www.sudantribune.com/spip.php?article63903

the other hands acted as if South Sudan was not a Sovereign nation. All of those created backlashes, and political activists from all walks of life blasted those who mishandled the matter.

In the march to nationhood, South Sudanese were overwhelmed by the responsibility for having to start a country from scratch. Like new countries around the world, South Sudan was born of numerous deadliest conflicts between north and south, and southerners themselves. The struggle for the liberation of South Sudan had never been easy, Southerners were fitted against themselves in many occasions, and scores of people have been lost as the wars raged. It took tribes in the South, clans and regions a chunk of their wealths and lives for the vision of a secular State in the South to be established.

While the problem of the Sudan was defined in the image of Southern's identity crisis, Sudan as a separate from the troubled South fell into the same trap where some regions in the Sudan; Dar Fur, central Sudan, Eastern Sudan and some select tribes in the north of Khartoum saw the same problem that South had identified prior the independence of the Sudan from Great Britain. The political enlightment spreadheaded by Southerns became the path that others in the Greater Sudan had follow when elites in the Sudan idolized national leadership, and pay no attention to good of the country as a whole.

CHAPTER SIX

The Wraths of the Self-Imposed War

The scourges of war, famine and disease destroyed old communities and identities, forced peoples to move, and created new communities out of survivors and refugees, often linked in unequal and dependent relations.[90]

War is too expensive, cost lives and destroys society. As South Sudan struggle to forge national identity, leaders were busy enriching themselves at the expense of the State. In countries emerging from violent conflict, the main political actors are generally strongly militarized. While non-militant political

---

90   Ethnicity, patronage and the African state: The politics of uncivil nationalism. (n.d). African Affairs, 97(388), 305-341. https://lopes.idm.oclc.org/login?url=http://search.ebscohost.com/login.aspx?direct=true&db=edswss&AN=000007559100001&site=eds-live&scope=site

parties may exist, many of the electoral competitors may be formerly armed actors who only recently became formal political parties (Brosche, & Hoglund, 2016). South Sudan as a country that emerged from violent conflict had not given democracy a chance, political parties are armed groups, with political aspirants seen of having taken up arms to cease political power once their peace deals are reached. For example, the first groups of political aspirants who took up are against the Government of Southern Sudan in 2010 relinquished rebelled once they were offered seats in the Government. It has been the cycle; young political aspirants now joins armed groups to rise to their potentials.

In the biggest armed conflict (2013) since independence, the rebels ended up asking for gubernatorial posts and other constitutional posts. What occurred in South Sudan after independence was the usual scene of the 20th century Africa, and it is more likely to be case in South Sudan. It is undisputed fact that fighting between factions loyal to President Salva Kiir and soldiers loyal Riek Machar pushed the country into a civil war and almost emptied the government's coffers. The economy has been struggling with hyper-inflation and soaring food and commodity prices- pushing many on the brink of hunger (Ashaba, Paalo, & Adu-Gyamfi, 2019).[91] The new conflict in South Sudan has spoiled South Sudanese diaspora desire to

91   Ashaba, Ivan & Paalo, Sebastian & Adu-Gyamfi, Samuel. (2019). State Fragility, Regime Survival and Spoilers in South Sudan. International Journal of African and Asiatic Studies. https://doi.org/10.13135/1825-263X/3319 https://www.researchgate.net/publication/333210572_State_Fragility_Regime_Survival_and_Spoilers_in_South_Sudan

return home because chance of one being able to make a living in the midst of the ongoing political strife are next to nothing. With that, South Sudanese born outside Africa are foreigners, and would not have the will to reconstruct a new society from scratch. It is going to be a tough invention of a livable society.

Since the voluminous National Dialogue has been in motion for many months, no conclusive reports on its success, it may be time for South Sudan to seek real solution to the conflict. For quite sometimes, people have been riding on the back of the President, some taking his right hand for enrichment only. Without declarative outcome, members of the Steering Committee need to absolve and retire into their daily activities. The mood of the crowds behind the scenes tells it all. There are times where decisions-making ought to be inclusive, especially where long-term things are at stake.

One of the many moral duties of the Rights based organizations is for them to push for transparency and accountability in governments. For quite some time, South Sudanese civil society organizations have been dubbed into being agencies of the Government of the day, chose to be inactive for few making a living, gave in to intimidation, not reporting on the things that should not be done the Government and agencies of the Government. The citizens of South Sudan continue to live in the shadow of their leaders, giving too much away in the name of supporting the people the love dearly. The leaders in return pays no attention to the plight on many people who live in absolutely poverty. There have been waves of power struggle among the former warlords, and they recruit from the home-villages, and builds the powerbase from bottom-up. For the most parts, internal politics is often the umbrella under which leaders based their decisions.

A long power struggle in South Sudan sparked off the crisis (civil war) just two years after the declaration of independence. The government's insistence on refuting the underlying causes of the conflict has stalled a peace process mediated by the Inter-Governmental Authority on Development (IGAD), leading to senseless killings, mass displacements, and a resurgence of ethnic hatred. The features of the internal conflict in South Sudan mirror one another's causes, bundled as different sets of variables grouped into three-loosely linked to ethnic heterogeneity, unequal distribution of natural resources, and State capacity.[92]

Role of Tribes in Political Anarchy

In the developing world, leaders rely on their localities, they often rally their ethnic groups to climb to the top or hang on to power. The ethnic based poltics is the biggest cancer in Africa, it has killed nationalism in many parts of Africa, including economic degradation. This has caused in enormous suffering and prolonged many conflicts. The incentive for leaders is the throne whiles the tribal or ethnic loyalists' only incentive is the priceless pride.

Many violent conflicts are fought between the members of different ethnic groups. Ethnicity allows for the clear

---

92   Logo MuLukwat, K. H. (2015). Challenges of Regulating Non-International Armed Conflicts - an Examination of Ongoing Trends in South Sudan's Civil War. Journal of International Humanitarian Legal Studies, 6(2), 414

differentiation of ingroups and outgroups, facilitating mobili-
zation to collective action. Thus, in divided societies, it is strate-
gically promising for competing political elites to rally support
on the basis of ethnic political agendas. Such exclusive political
agitation will likely trigger analogous reactions from other ethnic groups, potentially sparking an intergroup spiral of ethnic
radicalization.[93]

Most of the conflict with ethnic or tribal agendas ends up
in resolutions that do not really solve the problem, but rather preserve the grudges for all the coming generations. This is
evidented by the facts that oppositions reference their fathers'
and grandfathers' pasts, making an endless political redress. For
example, Kenya opposition leader Raila Odinga have been on
the stage for too long, and his supporters have been bathed in
all those happened during Jomo Kenyatta's time and Moi's era.

In Sudan, where northen Arabs through the ages have dom-
inated the state and deciminated the South fitting one black
African tribe against another, the said "aktul al-abidbilabid'---
"Kill the slave through the slave"[94]

93   De Juan, A. (2013). Devolving Ethnic Conflicts: The Role of Subgroup
Identities for Institutional Intergroup Settlements. Civil Wars, 15(1), 78. https://
doi-org.lopes.idm.oclc.org/10.1080/13698249.2013.781304.https://lopes.
idm.oclc.org/login?url=https://search.ebscohost.com/login.aspx?direct=true&d-
b=a9h&AN=87373928&site=eds-live&scope=site

94   Berkeley, Bill. (2001). Race, Tribe, and Power in the Heart of Africa. World Policy Journal, 18(1), 79. https://search-ebscohost-com.lopes.idm.oclc.
org/login.aspx?direct=true&db=edsjsr&AN=edsjsr.40209734&site=eds-live&-
scope=site

South Sudan's Revitalized Peace Agreement

Unlike anything that people in the vicinity of South Sudan have witnessed, South Sudanese gets caught up in a cycle of senseless lynchings, the results of political uneasiness wreckless at the highest level. Since the signing of CPA-2005, there have been petty conflicts in different regions of South Sudan, but the urban centers were untouched except Malakal where former Sudanese militias fought the SPLA in 2006 and 2009 respectively. The nature of wars sometimes don't get the attention of the world at large because the origin and the reason for staging such armed conflicts have been too remote. Between the period of 2006 and 2011, developments and repatration of South Sudanese from refugee camps have been disrupted, and people who have lived in foreign lands for many decades.

South Sudan has been more like a vacation resort for South Sudanese in East Africa and those in the diaspora. A generation has been lost in the two-decades ware between South Sudan and the Sudan. And more importantly, South Sudanese have lost their identity and pride in a thin air. Had crucial things been done, South Sudanese would have crafted their own identity based on their customs and traditional way of life. With the civil war that took considerable amount of time, there is even more loss in term of people's patriotism and willingness to start the country from scratch.

CHAPTER SEVEN

Social Activism in South Sudan

National leaders must rise above factions. Our leadership has been for so long viewed as reflective of factions rather than of the whole.[95]

Take it or leave it, it might have been a work of some cunts to put words in the mouth of President Salva Kiir, and for him to preside over the senseless conflict in the country. There is no way that a sensible person would believe that South Sudanese online chased away citizens from the homes in South Sudan. Shortly after the power wrangle in December 2013, many civilians died from the breakaway armies and the invading armies.

---

95   Deng, Francis Mading, forwarded by Kevin M. Cahill, Sudan at the Brink. Fordham University Press and the Institute for International Humanitarian Affairs, New York, 2010.

The South Sudanese society was caught in between melting rocks, no authority was in charge since the back and forth capturing of the garrison towns of Bortown, Bentiu and Malakal. If birds in the wild have long term memories of all the things that took place in the Republic of South Sudan, they would be the eye witnesses. It is unfortunate to recall that some regional leaders, particularly, the president of the Republic of Uganda aided the situation by taking side, and sent his army to pursuing the disgruntled SPLA's rebelling soldiers.

President Museveni of Uganda had this say: "Only the other day, 13 January, the SPLA [South Sudan army] and elements of our army had a big battle with these rebel troops at a point about 90 kilometres [55 miles] from Juba, where we inflicted a big defeat on them……Unfortunately, many lives were lost on the side of the rebels. We also took casualties and also had some dead."[96]

The episode is hard to believe, but the scale of displacement speaks for what actually went wrong in the Republic of South Sudan. The incidents recorded, and testimonies from the survivors of the war, and across the spectrum will fill volumes of untitled books. In the previous conflicts: 1955-1972 and 1983-2005, the number of people displaced from their homes, and into refugee camps have never reached the figures at hand. There have been instances where the president blamed the social media commentators for the mass displacement, but intentional observers who have been dealing with the nation's leadership have

---

96   BBC. (January 16, 2014). Yoweri Museveni: Uganda troops fighting South Sudan rebels. https://www.bbc.com/news/world-africa-25759650

different version: "Kiir is the heart of the problem," Princeton Lyman, US former Envoy to South Sudan & Sudan. How can the President be the heart of problems in South Sudan when his presidential decrees are cheered as popular demands by the people?

In the last couple of years, Advocacy Groups, particularly the South Sudanese civil society organizations outside the country have done a terrific job, and by relaying the situation as it unfolded. There is no better eye than that of an informed person, and reflecting of a person who grew up knowing nothing, but war. The hardships associated working in a volatile nation like the Republic of South Sudan don't call for giving up or not saying things that can help in the structural reform of the Government and in the development of legal mechanisms.

A while back, Deng Athuai, and before the South Sudanese civil war started, the then head of South Sudan's Alliance of civil societies organizations was kidnapped at gunpoint, taken to unknown location, locked into a bag and dumped in the nearby bushes. Not long before the first incident, Deng Athuai was fired at, wounded and returned fire in self defense. Thereafter, he was relieved and replaced with person who would do nothing, but condone policies that hurt the country and wellbeing of the citizens in the world's youngest nation. The people who are the faces of South Sudan have little or nothing to offer to the coming generations of South Sudanese. It's often considered futile and unfortunate for people to strike at the system that failed the nation, but bitter truths have to be placed in an open air-market. Those who have eyes will read by themselves, and those with unbiased intellect will take serious notes and envision a better way forward.

In the face of all the challenges in South Sudan, very small groups of people have the will to push the Government and law enforcement agencies to be mindful of respecting people's rights as enshrined in the South Sudan's Interim Constitution. It is of a great value that people be treated humanely, and all people properties and interests be protected equally. Land and real property are very crucial things in the world, and almost none existing in South Sudan. Traditionally, land was owned by tribes, clans and sections. People who are born in those units have natural rights to the land and its use. Comes the moderns South Sudan, the Government defined lands: Private lands, community lands and public lands.

In the South Sudan societies, property ownership and inheritance follow certain community's norms. It is recognizing most South Sudanese have the back-home ways for looking at things. The gender roles are pretty much in their traditional form, and things will take the shape of modern time once customary laws have been integrated and polished to meets the standards of this centuries. Rural South Sudanese communities have two sets of narratives about how women can live good lives—a set which they characterize as traditional and a set which they characterize as modern (LeRoux-Rutledge, 2020). With the independence of South Sudan, and the returned of refugees from all around the world, South Sudan is struggling to accommodate all the South Sudanese, in term of meets people's expectations and the demands for living in the urban centers. There has been influx of foreigners into the countries for the purpose of doing business, and those foreign residents of South Sudan do not fall into the category of South Sudanese. There is a need for some changes to be made, and that require rapid examinations of the pasts notes and the current affairs. This would means taking measures that would safeguard against keeping women in the old cocoons.

Women's equality and empowerment are international development priorities but are difficult to achieve. Much gender and development literature blames entrenched "traditional" gender roles and norms, using them to explain slow progress towards gender and development goals, such as girls' and women's education, women's participation in public decision-making, and women's land and property ownership.[97]

In order to have an equitable society, South Sudanese need to make some reforms, and modernize some things that were revered and left in the hands of traditional authorities. For example, chiefs, more so than other customary authorities, had always held intermediary positions, historically playing a central role in both local government structures and networks of kinship and patronage, while their precise responsibilities depended both on their capacities to successfully claim legitimacy

97   LeRoux-Rutledge, E. (2020). Re-evaluating the "traditional": How the South Sudanese use established gender narratives to advance women's equality and empowerment. World Development, 132, N.PAG. https://doi-org.lopes.idm.oclc.org/10.1016/j.worlddev.2020.104929.   https://lopes.idm.oclc.org/login?url=https://search.ebscohost.com/login.aspx?direct=true&db=ehh&AN=143419297&site=eds-live&scope=site&custid=s8333196&groupid=main&profile=eds1

'downward' as community representatives and 'upward' as extensions of higher-level governing authorities.[98]

After the war ended in 2005, South Sudanese who had fled the country for more two decades started to have sense of wanting to return home. That desire to go repatriate to South Sudanse had its own challenges; moving in a place that one had not lived for almost a generation is bumpy. Also, there were children born in foreign lands, they never had a place to call home; only lived in foreign countries in a refugee camps. There were no attachments to the countries they were born and raised into nor did they have the sense of their ancestral lands. With all the doubts, most people were repatriated by the UNHCR to places they referred as homes. These places were either bushy they have been occupied by others who moved into their areas deserted. At that juncture, contest over lands become a major problem that Southern Sudanese, later South Sudan Government had to deal with as most disagreements over lands ended deadly. The contestation over land and its governance extended also to the rural areas surrounding the town, where displacement had left the pre-war boundaries between plots and communities in disarray, resulting in disagreement about which clan held land

98   Van De Kerkhof, Marlie, Mathijs Van Leeuwen, and Yves Van Leynseele. 2018. "Transforming Land Governance and Strengthening the State in South Sudan." African Affairs 117 (467): 286–309. https://search-ebscohost-com.lopes. idm.oclc.org/login.aspx?direct=true&db=edb&AN=129289279&site=eds-live&-scope=site

and governing authority.[99] There had been little resolution such disagreement as the governments, states, local and central government has adequate resources to modernize customary law and practice that governed much of the land, but have not be incorporated into states' constitutions, and educate the civil population the importance of adhering to the federal laws of the land.

The State of South Sudan had dealing with intercommunal feuds plus rebellions for much of its self-governing as well as independence period, 2011-2021. This is not to ignore the fact that land governance is an important doorway for both state and non-state local public authorities to expand their power and authority at the local level. It is through dealing with land attribution and dispute resolution that local public authorities may establish or consolidate their power, (re)gain legitimacy, and generate local people's confidence and trust.[100] For an land to have value, it has been regulated and managed in a way that benefits both the owners and the society as a whole. Lands can change ownership, but within the framework by the lands' laws. CHAPTER II of the South Sudan's Constitution (2011) defines

99   Van De Kerkhof, Marlie, Mathijs Van Leeuwen, and Yves Van Leynseele. 2018. "Transforming Land Governance and Strengthening the State in South Sudan." African Affairs 117 (467): 286–309. https://search-ebscohost-com.lopes. idm.oclc.org/login.aspx?direct=true&db=edb&AN=129289279&site=eds-live&-scope=site

100   Van De Kerkhof, Marlie, Mathijs Van Leeuwen, and Yves Van Leynseele. 2018. "Transforming Land Governance and Strengthening the State in South Sudan." *African Affairs 117 (467): 286–309.* https://search-ebscohost-com.lopes.idm.oclc.org/login.aspx?direct=true&db=ed-b&AN=129289279&site=eds-live&scope=site

land ownership, Tenure, and Natural Resources as follows:

170. Land Ownership:

1. All land in South Sudan is owned by the people of South Sudan and its usage shall be regulated by the government in accordance with the provisions of this Constitution and the law.

2. Notwithstanding sub-Article (1) above, and the provisions of Article 28 of this Constitution, the government at all levels, may expropriate land in the public interest as shall be prescribed by law.

171. Land Tenure

1. The regulation of land tenure, usage and exercise of rights thereon shall be governed by this Constitution and the law.

2. Without prejudice to sub-Article (4) below, the land tenure system in South Sudan shall consist of:

   a. *public land;*

   b. *community land; and*

   c. *private land.*

3. Public land shall include, but not be limited to:

   a. *all land owned, held, or otherwise acquired by any level of government as*

   defined by law; and

   b. *all land which is not otherwise classified as community or private.*

4. Regardless of the classification of the land in question, rights over all

subterranean and other natural resources throughout South Sudan, including petroleum and gas resources and solid minerals, shall belong to the National Government and shall be regulated by law.

5. Community land shall include all lands traditionally and historically held or used by local communities or their members. They shall be defined, held, managed and protected by law.

6. Private land shall include:

a. registered land held by any person under leasehold tenure in accordance with the law.

b. investment land acquired under lease from the Government or community for purposes of social and economic development in accordance with the law; and

c. any other land designated as private land by law.

7. Rights in land and resources owned, held, or otherwise acquired by the Government shall be exercised through the appropriate or designated level of government which shall recognize customary land rights under customary land law.

8. All levels of government shall institute a process to progressively develop and amend the relevant laws to incorporate customary rights and practices and local heritage.

9. Communities and persons enjoying rights in land shall be consulted in decisions that may affect their rights in lands and resources.

10. Communities and persons enjoying rights in land shall be entitled to prompt and equitable compensation on just terms arising from acquisition or development of land in

their areas in the public interest.[101]

The land laws as defined by the supreme law of the land has to be adhered, and changes made. There more benefits in following through with the law as written, disputed over who own can be resolved consist with what the law says. Much works remain to be done, but achievable.

Activism has no Boundaries

On the height of the South Sudan civil war (2013-2014), John Ngong Aluong also known as Jon Penn trekked to the Rebels' camp in the remote Jonglei, and was able to spend time with Dr. Riek Machar and Dak Kueth, the Magician who was heavily relied on by the then newly formed armed rebellion. When the photo surfaced on the social media, possibly by John Penn de Ngong himself, people from his home area (Bor) took to the cyberspace, and attacked John Penn de Ngong relentlessly. This wasn't the everyday rant, it was something serious because many people were slaughtered in Bortown and Akoba by the rebels' associates. To make things even worse, Jon Penn de Ngong did the same, and took the social media with his seasoned political arguments.

At the course of protecting his image, he wrote countless posts, and defended his reasons for traveling to Pagak. The attack raged, but John Penn de Ngong kept up with the attack,

---

101   Constitute. The World's Constitutions to read, search, and compare. South Sudan Constitution (2011), retrieved on November 23, 2021, from https://www.constituteproject.org/constitution/South_Sudan_2011.pdf

and made sure that his place of residence is not infiltrated by those who thought he has done the most unthinkable. Like John Penn de Ngong, most people who have prior knowledge of the dirty dealing did not buy the "attempted coup" narrative, and for reasons given by independent analysts. While the continued, South Sudanese who supported Government and rebels created more enemies than anyone could imagine. The daily social media blasting, character assassination, and intimidation lasted for more than expected.

The Government and the rebels alike waged senseless war. The conflict resulted into maiming of too many people, displaced millions according United Nation High Commissioner for Refugee (UNHCR), and nation's only source of revenue (Oil) was brought to its knee. Years later, John Penn de Ngong recovered his reputation as a nationalist, a writer who keep things cool, and he was able to publish the recollections he put together during the war. His visit to Addis Ababa, the Peace's venue was outstanding. The delegates were able to buy few of his public, and many were seen showing off with copies of John Penn's books.

With all the due respects to Peace Activists and Human Rights Advocate, those who squarely protect the rights of underprivileged and the most vulnerable members of the any society must be given credits for their works. And as a result, John Penn de Ngong is one of the few nationalists who know keep things under control. As South Sudanese, we must listen to our own voices, response other's people opinions, and treat ourselves with respect. The ongoing war has caused too many lives, destroyed too many properties, and dismantled social relationships because too many people were pushed for the edge for political reasons. Preach peace, preach what you practice, and lead by example.

CHAPTER EIGHT

Forging the Nation's Future Together

With regard to historical diversity, Garang went back to the history of Sudan and Ancient Egypt (which is interconnected with Sudan) to find an anchor in history, because the past of a nation also plays a role in determining its future. In this context, he refers to the various peoples and kingdoms that thrived and disappeared in the geographical area that constitutes the present-day Sudan. In this sense,the vision has strong historical and contemporary foundations. The New Sudan vision aims at establishing a state on both the historical diversity and the contemporary plurality of Sudan.[102]

Had Garang's Successor (Pres. Salva Kiir Mayardit) followed

---

102   Nasredeen, A. (2013). Identities and citizenship in Sudan: Governing constitutional principles. African Human Rights Law Journal, (2), 383.

his footsteps or the SPLM's founding principles, things would have reached the heights they have reached after the independence of South Sudan. There is much to applying the Vision of New Sudan than people normally things. The vision would have shaded light on the new Republic, and bringing the people of South Sudan with a fresh energy. In the bush, people were eagered to have a new beginning, and that was not necessary having the united Sudan, but having policies that treat citizens equally, and akin nation's composition. For what the nation of South Sudan means to citizens who never had a nationstate, the generation of freedom-fighters should just quit politics, retire into their villages, and let the former child soldiers who are in their early 40s handle the nation's affairs.

The nation of South Sudan has bled for too long, the citizens have been subjected to unbearable suffering and economic hardships. In the face of these tragic circumstances, there is an urgent need for a sustainable peace and for a robust reconciliation process that can unite South Sudanese toward a resumption of national development and consolidation (Modi, Opongo, & Smith, 2019).[103] It takes contemporaries for nations to achieve their potentials; South Sudan is being run by old schools, and their approach to world's current challenges is not upto date.

---

103   Modi, L. P., Opongo, E. O., & Smith, R. D. (2019). South Sudan's Costly Conflict and the Urgent Role of Religious Leaders. The Review of Faith & International Affairs, 17(2), 37–46. https://doi-org.lopes.idm. oclc.org/10.1080/15570274.2019.1608660.   https://lopes.idm.oclc.org/log-in?url=https://search.ebscohost.com/login.aspx?direct=true&db=rfh&AN=AT-LAiA14190617000293&site=eds-live&scope=site&custid=s8333196&groupid=-main&profile=eds1

There have been number of setbacks to prove unreliability of the current leaders.

After 8 years of tearing the country apart, turning tribes against themselves, borrowing recklessly, making nation's highways as shooting ranches and making major towns large prisons, the woes want to renegotiate their way back in the looting pipe. In every country, there are people who take the backseat, and be advisors on important things in the country. The political clowns who hijacked the 2015 Agreement for the Resolution Conflict in South Sudan (ARCISS) have archaic thoughts, they have themselves in a resolution meant to return the country to normalcy. They are the same groups of paranoid warlords who cannot spend a day without a job, and they rather destroy the country than look for tractors and plough their lands.

Much of the political unrests seen in the Sub-Saharan Africa, South Sudan in particular is mostly catalyzed by thirst for quick wealth and unlimited political powers. Some people may agree that the old guards are no longer capable of resolving political differences, and planning for the nation's future. The war is being fought by their children and grand children, most whom are riding on the backs of obsolete politicians. It's painful to watch a whole generation being lost, opportunities being domino and resources being wasted for a war that would be a shame to have in history books. If you want to hear voices of the suffering South Sudanese, then tune in the emerging leaders' hotline, adopt and adept to the rhythms, and follow the crowds.

Solution to South Sudan's Military & Political Unrests

In order to end the violence across South Sudan, a well crafted mechanisms need to be in place. The elites must rise above tribal traps; they need to build institutions, setup academic channels whereby younger generations would be able to shape their future. The structure of the government agreed upon whether via negotiated peace agreement or through the National legislative Assembly must be adhered to. The nation of South Sudan has been floating for too long, more than a decade in transition is too elastic, and is partially responsible for the political and military chaos that ensued.

A shift in political strategy is badly needed, amendments instead of interim Constitution must be the bases upon which new laws and rules must emerge. The nation's appeared to have abused their powers through the lack of static rules. Recommended, at some points, during and before the end Transitional period, South Sudanese all over the world will have to define how the next few years would look like. The political situation in the country appears too fluids, not even the custodians of the national Government are in charge of the programs and the many function of the State.

The Region and the international community have been shown to possess some sorts of interests in the affairs of South Sudan. The wrangling among the warring factions, oppositions and the citizens is far more challenging than could be imagine. The little known fact about the South Sudanese political establishment is not helping the country to move away from the tribal pendulum and the immaturity shown by the unlearned warlords who always exhibit improper tendency to destroy their own country at the expense of their foreign Advisors. Given the unstable political platform, each and every political has at least a foreign element with vested interest.

The citizens of South Sudan have fallen victims, the natural wealth that they sits on is being drained by unknown in investors, shoddy contracts that benefited the initiators of war have been heard afar. When the SPLA was in the bush, the centrifugal forces of the Sudd were as much a challenge to collective action as an asset inhibiting state control; now that it occupied the seat of power, this fragmented ecology, inhabited by just as intractable socio-political groups, also became a potential site of challenge to its rule (Schouten, & Bachmann, 2020). The endowment in the form of all sort of minerals and the oil Reserve turned out to be cursed onto the indigenous Africans whose life was dependent on agriculture and livestock. Little is left for all the coming generations to enjoy, ethnic tensions flourished, and politics of divide and rule have taken toll on the civil population for the obvious known reasons.

South Sudanese Community-Based Organizations

At home and around the world, South Sudanese are better know through through community based organizations. When political structures have been parked, people resort to associations as the haven for political activities. Prior to South Sudan gaining independence, South Sudanese from all walks of life maintained their social and cultural cohension through associations and church's organizations. In diaspora, internal displaced camps and refugee camps, South Sudanese formed and run associations, most of which helped the needy. In order for such organizations to operate and functions, elections have been the basis for bringing volunteers to powers. The charters and structures have been designed more like political institutions, and aspiring leaders use political slogans to get support from the people in the communities.

Over the years, South Sudanese associated have grown beyond political parties in the Republic of South Sudan, and leaders are more reputable than members of partlimants in the new Republic. With tribes being the basis of everything in South Sudan, and rest of Africa, the community based organizations (CBOs) are formed based on tribes and clans, people who run them are from portion within those entities. Because nothing is working in South Sudan, the well to do, well educated and energetic young leaders have been lured by political conditions to seek refuge in the location organizations. For them to keep up with forces of the modern world, few of them picked up political lines, and campaigned for positions in the CBOs. The campaigned and activities of the locals CBOs have caught attentions of the South Sudanese, turning campaigns for volunteer work into political rallies, and nonfunctioning State's apparatuses taking interest in the activities. In the recent years, people of supposed middle age (35-44) have been seen volunteering their times and resources for local community-based associations.

In the United States, Australia and South Sudan's youth

association political rallies have sown new seeds for democracy in the country. Although it is a good thing to invest in nonprofit organizations, putting the entire generations on a volunteerly is a majot drawback. Most of these young men and women who are supposed to be in Government dispatching important functions of Government have been reduced to puppets of the non-existing political spectrum. The paradym of building a country from local materials is disappearing. It would be surprising to see the best South Sudanese politicians are from the dotcom generation, and they are only known from their social and political activism. When one of the youth association political rallies campaign was held in Juba (Twic East Youth Association), the country as a whole paid a great deal activities that were being streamed via facebook videos. The able and best South Sudanese leaders are among the generation that was born or raised duting the wartime. But because of the squeezed and restrictive political space, most of these young men and women have been reduced to being leaders of the local associations, most which are pouring into money for the vulnerable.

The real social development and political change will come once these energetic people are allowed a space to stretch their muscles, compete freely with people of their calibre and given full protection to move the country to the next level. There is no doubt, majority of the South Sudanese politicking on the social media have acquired world's standard education, and they are out in the field to deliver if offered the opportunity to spearhead the needed change. It is worth noting that South Sudanese who were resettled in the developed nations some two decades are in a hung because of political crisis in South Sudan. This is so because majority of them have never accepted their resettled countries as their second, and they committed their resources and visions for people who were left in the refugee camps as well as those who remained in South Sudan's villages.

It take generosity for people lifted out of desperation. The South Sudanese who were resettled in the developed nations of the West committed more than ¾ of their earnings for the betterment of people in Africa, hoping to return home one day and make positive impact both socioeconomic and political impact. As much as realities of the political condition in the country are concern, it is more than an illusion. And surely, time wasted can never be recovered. Every unprecedented political move in South Sudan has occupied its own space as part of the history.

Progressive Thinking

Forging national identity is a product of cohesive agendas. For all the reasons analyzed throughout the book, South Sudanese have hard time appreciating their national identity. The progressive and reformist thinkers have difficulties consolidating their basis and moving the nation ideologically. The think-tanks are yet to realize how much they would contribute to the nation of South Sudan; some are floating while others are soulsearching where to draw the line. States do nation building by integrating their ethnic groups, usually through coercion. Sometimes, ethnic groups benefit from integration such as opportunities for better jobs. (Tepfenhart, 2013).[104] This can only be achieved if the Government adopted merits-based employment and guaranteeing that citizens enjoy equitable access to jobs. As citizens enjoys fruits of their nations equally, there will be peace and tranquility in the country.

The groups of young entreprenuers, social and political activists are at their prime time to form clubs that would have positive impacts on the nation's education system, economy and politics. The country as a whole did not have enough courage to open up space for such to operate freely. Everything in the Republic of South Sudan is seen in term of politics; things are often in face value, people in power are overacted to their maximums whenever they address what would be a very simple thing. The goes the same way to those who holds no political posts or known wealth; they are underestimated and seen as lesser to contribute anything to the nation and state building.

Families at the Crossroad

In the midst of political crises in South Sudan, odds things happened. The very families built from scratch, of course during the war of liberation have been over their throats over petty disagreement. The fact that everything has been disorganized, people from across the country have had their bad days and good

---

104   Tepfenhart, M. (2013). The Causes of Ethnic Conflicts. Comparative Civilizations Review, 68, 84–97. https://lopes.idm.oclc.org/login?url=https://search.ebscohost.com/login.aspx?direct=true&db=ofs&AN=87591213&site=eds-live&-scope=site&custid=s8333196&groupid=main&profile=eds1

days. When the vehicles swerved off the road, freshable ideas crashed, and the delicious dispersed off the paved road. There was not much left, so things that would have not come to sight were unintentionally exposed. The dining table politics became everyone business. With many political camps, and very little hope for reconciliation, everyone went about his/her choice. One of the Dinka's saying has it that, " I go where I'm liked." It cannot be more truer than when South Sudanese where hunting themselves at every corner in South Sudan, in neighboring countries, and on the social media.

When the manificiently matured fish fought over the last shell of coral reef, the rocks suffered greatly. More the the fiction than the reality, families who fought to protect their hard earned privilege blended into opposing groups, became completely disconnected, and spoke in tongue while they chase the monster to the unknown destination. Before anyone know it, the people whom many look up to for direction switched sides overnight, and when silence. There was a social media meniac as families took to the facebook and other social media platform, defaming themselves, writing articles and shitchating to the world within their reach.

From the getgo, there was no formidable reason to set the whole country ablaze. The politics gonewild caught many citizens offguard, and by the time the unweaned politicians reached their bases, the guns were already aimed at unknown targets. Of the many unbecoming stories, three stood the course of madness: two cousins have their nieces and nephew mowed their names and themselves on the social media, posting craps belittling their opposing views; a wife of prominent soldier of all times defected to Government, and started to talk shit about her husband who had lost much of his wealth and the support from his home state. And the third case scenarios is when a son and a mother stayed in different political camps while their supporters and opponents exchange nasting insults. The final episode is when a lady who fought every literate opposed to the Government on the social media turned agains the same Government after she was denied access to some political amenities.

The explosion cause massive displays on the social media, people who have been vilified and victimized by the very same lady watched passionately, and as she dropped bunch of booms July House, often referred to as J1. The supposedly brave woman of all times shockingly said things no ever thought would be said by the very same person. *The readers and the viewers split into more than five groups: angry mobs, waterless sympasizers, tearful clowns, guilty associates and bumpy riders.* It was a moment that many have not anticipated because everything has been black and white to her. The victims of her vilifications will remain speechless as long as she live. After all, based has collapsed, so nothing is to be honored or celebrated.

Politics and Sports

South Sudanese doesn't have a nationwide population sport. For the past 10 years, the nation struggled between turnbuckles. There have been no stability for the country to modernize some of its traditional sports. For example, wrestling is popular among the Jiengs and the Lotuho in Eastern Equatoria. Although the sport has survived the rapidity of the western's popular culture, it's yet to be upgraded. The sport almost picked up in 2010, but the autonomous region was rocked by inter-tribal fighting and rebellion following the dispute of the Sudan's general election where some former warlords accused the ruling party, the Sudan's People Liberation Movement(SPLM) of having rigged the election in favor of its preferred members. The rebels and the splinter groups were either defeated or persuaded to sign a peace with the Sudan's Government after the official secession of the country from the Sudan.

After quite sometimes of infighting, the calm returned, but the first ever presidential election in the independent South Sudan was hanging in the air. The mistrust within the SPLM led to another, yet a destructive civil war. With the sporadic fighting all over true country, every activity, sport and trading were halted by the war. When the Revitalized peace agreement was rejuvenated, there was some hopes for the real normalcy to come back.

In 2020, wrestling between counties in Lakes State and Jonglei's counties was restarted. The first few matches when okay, and there was even a greater need to have wrestling as a match among South Sudan's grand regions(Bahr El Ghazal, Equatoria and Upper Nile). The first ever regional wrestling tournament was cancelled, the circumstances were very murky. Again, in 2021, the match between Greater Bahr El Ghazal and Greater Upper Nile was set to be on July 31, 2021. Like everything in South Sudan, the match drew too much attention. The Greater Upper Nile Team paid a visited to first vice President, Dr. Riek Machar, who happen to be from Unity state of the Greater Upper Nile. Quickly, but relentlessly, the Greater Bahr El Ghazal Team was invited by the nation's First Lady, Ayen Mayardit. With that, the dynamics of the wrestling had changed colors, and it was no longer a regular match. The coaches and the leaders of the two Teams agreed a venue, which was to be in Juba's Sherikhat, a suburb east of the White Nile.

Following hours of shooting and shouting on the social media, the Body that called itself Bahr El Ghazal wrestling association called a meeting, which reportedly lasted many hours. After the conclusion of that meeting, the secretaries of the Bahr El Ghazal wrestling association took the news media, and announced that they have cancelled the wrestling because they don't want to go to Shirikhat. The claimed put forth was that, their fans and the more than 7000 vehicles that they expect to cross the Juba's bridge to Shirikhat could make it on time.

Therefore, they have decided to cancel the match, unless South Sudan wrestling federation agree to change the venue to New-site, Juba's west suburb which they claimed to have the capacity for this kind of tournament. The reactions and outbursts during and after the live coverage of the announcement could be heard from Heaven. The long awaited wrestling was canceled a day away from the agreed date. Politics has been elevated to higher level in the Republic of South Sudan. Anything that has fans is politicized, not just in South Sudan, but worldwide. The difference is that, South Sudanese are yet to take commentaries and criticism likely. Unlike deities which were the traditional sources of divine powers, imported religions enthrenched into political territorie.

Religions and Governance

It has been recorded through the ages that religion is a catalyst in many conflicts if not all. In around 1000 BCE, the Arabs from the Midlands, now known as the Middle entered SUDAN via the Red Sea and the Egypt's southern corridor. These people arrived as long distance traders, guided by the religious beliefs as their form of imperialism.

The Arabs first came to North Africa in ap proximately 1000 BCE, but their immigration from the Arabian Peninsula to the region intensified in the second half of the 1st millennium CE, and to Sudan – at the turn of the 1st and 2nd millenia CE. Islam was spreading along with the Arabs, who initially established considerable presence in the northeast regions of mod ern Sudan bordering the Red Sea, as well as in the valley of the Nile, penetrating further and further south along the river. By the late 15th – early 16th centuries CE, the political and economic apex of African civilization in the region was to be found in the sultanates of Darfur and Sennar, which successfully resisted Arab encroachment but adopted the religion and, to a certain extent, the language of the latter.[105]

The Arabs brought to Africa processed salt, iron ornaments, and weapons of various kinds. Those articles were exchanged in barter trade. They took with them things that they did not own, and Africans took from them things they don't have the technology to make. As time passed by, some traders, tired of long commutes and dangerous caravans, decided to make some opened lands as their homes. They set up camps, thatched houses with local building materials, started schools(madaras). The teaching in those schools were almost purely religious based teachings. They also started to teach locals the art of writing as well as some fundamental scriptures in the Quran. That was a turning point in planting new religion in African.

Elsewhere in the lives of the indigenous communities, everything takes the shape of God in the highest. The people from the new world have their own interests in additions to the religions that they carried with them in Holy Texts. The Africans, particularly the Sudanese down South resisted quite a number of odd things. It was observed that:

Islam is advancing in the Sudan in some parts rapidly, in others more slowly, and it is advancing by peaceful propaganda. It is this peaceful penetration which Christian missions must meet, and therefore the sources of its success are matters which demand thought as well as mere expression. Islam is advancing

105   Kostelyanets, S. V. (2021). The Rise and Fall of Political Islam in Sudan. Politikologija Religije, 15(1), 85–104. https://lopes.idm.oclc.org/login?url=https://search.ebscohost.com/login.aspx?direct=true&db=rfh&AN=ATLAiAZI210510000126&site=eds-live&scope=site&custid=s8333196&groupid=-main&profile=eds1

more rapidly than Christianity, and if that advance is to be checked it must be understood. It is futile to imagine that it can be checked by methods designed for a very different warfare, a warfare against a paganism which was not advancing but perishing.[106]

Toward the mid portion of the 19th century, Europeans arrived with Christianity, and the same way a guiding star for colonialism. The two odd religions (Christianity and Islam) influenced African thinking, shaped political views as as well skewed cultures. By 1898, Turks have had enough of the resistance, and British were already in some parts of Africa doing exploration. In between, African tribes were engaged in petty violence, mostly fighting in the interests of their masters. That was unequivocally a replica of the schism in Europe when Christianity split along ideological lines. The same was true of the Islam when the two prominent scholars divided the religion into follow of Ali and follow of Muhammad. In the case of Sudanese, *the impact of Islam on the riverain northern Sudan was complex and cannot be simplistically reduced to a model of 'popular' or Sufi Islam in contrast to urban Azhari orthodoxy. The dominant state of the region between 1500 to 1800, the Funj Sultanate of Sinnār,*

---

106   Allen, R. (1920). Islam and Christianity in the Sudan. International Review of Mission, 9(4), 531–543. https://lopes.idm.oclc.org/login?url=https://search.ebscohost.com/login.aspx?direct=true&db=rfh&AN=ATLAiA14180731000930&site=eds-live&scope=site&custid=s8333196&groupid=main&profile=eds1

was both an African 'divine kingship' state and an Islamic polity.[107]

Fasting forward, Sudanese after the British left took very harsh routes toward running the country. The minority Muslims in the north, roughly about 11% that time, and 17% by 1981 assumed the total ownership of the country and its people. Many decades later, the form of Christianity in Africa became the opposite of radical Islam. The churches and their teachings assumed much work of the local authorities; government became inseparable from the church. While Christianized Africans cried marginalization from Islamic governments in the Sudan, the took radical approach in eradicating traditional beliefs, and at the same time taking from the people and giving none back. The enlightened minorities who saw irregularities in the way churches are run kept quite because majority blindly followed corrupt cults and not seeing the negative impact of such practices.

As urbanization becomes the new reality, citizens from around the country became Christians by default, and church leaders grew even much greediest than the biblical teachings. The offering and proceeds of the church became private properties of individuals and their allies within the systems. The ranks and files of church leaders started to dislike themselves, created chaos and the populous joined the drama, which then fragmented the church. With the proliferation and sophistication

---

107   O'Fahey, R. S. (1996). Islam and Ethnicity in the Sudan. Journal of Religion in Africa, 26(3), 258–267. https://lopes.idm.oclc.org/log-in?url=https://search.ebscohost.com/login.aspx?direct=true&db=rfh&AN=AT-LA0001015901&site=eds-live&scope=site&custid=s8333196&groupid=main&-profile=eds1

of communication technology, the unrest within the church reached a boiling pointless.

Leadership Without Social Responsibility

There are convincing reasons why South Sudan should not be in a state of disaster it is in right now. Competition for power radicalized by ethnic overtones has brewed nothing but catastrophe. South Sudan should realize that many if not all African countries are made up of different political parties and different "tribal" affiliations. This makes it important to have leadership that is thoughtful of the plight of the citizens, leadership that tolerates divergent political views and leadership that respects life (Mutanda, 2019).[108]

For one, leaders in South Sudan do not see the value of ethic, and responsibility to deliver services to the governed. The is not only in the Government but across all the social institutions in the country. With that, the focus is on the Government, and what people perceived as working for the people. In the most cases, leaders take attendance as satisfactory to the job they are assigned to do. One would argue for decades, especially with current leaders, and they will never understand what leadership is about. For lack of a better descriptive word, South Sudan's

---

108   Mutanda, D. (2019). The Centrality of Conflict Transformation in Solving Political Struggles and Political Violence in South Sudan. Strategic Review for Southern Africa, 41(1). https://lopes.idm.oclc.org/login?url=https://search.ebscohost.com/login.aspx?direct=true&db=edsgao&AN=eds-gcl.602243269&site=eds-live&scope=site&custid=s8333196&groupid=-main&profile=eds1

officials misunderstood what it means to be a leader; some takes arriving at work each day as a service-delivery. The social of clubs of chess and cards continue to be the common meetpoints.

In all of the public offices, leaders are too reluctant, and not accountable to the public. There is some sort of impunity that is not within the legal parameters. Most of the leaders see positions in Government as entitlements rather than a call fo serve the society. The truth to the matter is, leaders have no desire to leave behind a legacy by positively impacting public programs. The country has been plagued by social illnesses called corruption. People, whether in the rebells' camps or in Government have no genuine hearts to reform the society.

At the prime time when South Sudanese needed help, politicians and aspiring politicians took disastrous routes. At the end of the civil war, the nation's parliament topped 550 members of the parliament. It was the highest recorded legislative assembly, given the size of South Sudan among other nations of the world. The wrangles did not stopped in the nation's parliament, other social institutions disingenuously copycatted, and everything become a race for gain. The opportunists who laid in wait took positions in oppositions' allotments, and became national and states' members of the parliaments while others became counties' commissioners.

Conclusion

The overall theme of the THE DISCONNECTS: Tribes, Governance, and Power in South Sudan is about how the people in government really want to be seen, and the kind of life they want to lead. For the most parts, enemy from within is created by the improper use of tribal identity, system of governance and misuse of State's power. South Sudan is no exception from rest of the world; the problems of the world lies in use of people's power, race, resources, and religion to some extent. It happen that South Sudan's has its problem deeply rooted in tribal perspections, the way they have been governed since the Turkish time. The breakdown of the South Sudanese social institutions and religious institutions, which has now engulfed the country in hard to break toxic politics can all be blamed on the political setup. The continued identity crises and misconceptions create mistrust among the South Sudanese communities from all walks of life.

The country has gone through vicious cycle of conflicts; which led to loss of precious lives, mass displacement skyrocketed and too many opportunities have been lost over the course of the past four years. It may not may be the right thing to point finger at this juncture in the history of the young nation, but asking the leaders in charge to let the nation go into the hand of the younger ones may be the best option ever. There is a huge generational gap between the governed and the Rulers. The elites in that regard have lost grip of their powers, and leaders' methods for addressing social issues is not compatible with contemporary running of modern nation-states. The governed are either not complying with laws of the land or leaders are deploying wrong diagnostic strategies, and keeps using imporper methods to address the real political and social issues at hand.

SELECTED BIBLIOGRAPHY

A Abushouk, Ahmed Ibrahim. (2010). The Anglo-Egyptian Sudan: From Collaboration Mechanism to Party Politics, 1898–1956. *The Journal of Imperial and Commonwealth History Vol. 38, No. 2, June 2010, pp. 207–236.* https://www.academia. edu/3723516/

Aglionby, J. (2016). New conflict in South Sudan feared. *The Financial Times.* https://lopes.idm.oclc.org/login?url=http://search.ebscohost.com/login.aspx?direct=true&db=edsgbe&AN=edsgcl.464964185&site=eds-live&scope=site

Akol, Lam. SPLM/SPLA, The Nasir Declaration. *iUniverse,Inc., 2003.*

Alfred, Okech. (2007). Africa Peace Forum Regional Security, Gender Identity, and CPA Implementation in Sudan. *Africa Peace Forum and Project Ploughshares.* https://www.academia.edu/5007051/Africa_Peace_Forum_Regional_Security_Gender_Identity_and_CPA_Implementation_in_Sudan?email_work_card=view-paper

Alier, Abel. Southern Sudan: Too Many Agreements Dishonoured.New York: *Ithaca Press, 1990.*

Allen, R. (1920). Islam and Christianity in the Sudan. *International Review of Mission, 9(4), 531–543.* https://lopes.idm.oclc.org/login?url=https://search.ebsco-host.com/login.aspx?direct=true&db=rfh&AN=AT-LAiA14180731000930&site=eds-live&scope=site&cus-tid=s8333196&groupid=main&profile=eds1

Arop, Madut-Arop. Sudan's Painful Road to Peace. A Full Story of the Founding and Development of the SPLM/SPLA. *BookSurge, LLC., 2006.*

Ashaba, Ivan & Paalo, Sebastian & Adu-Gyamfi, Samuel. (2019). State Fragility, Regime Survival and Spoilers in South Sudan. *International Journal of African and Asiatic Studies.* https://doi.org/10.13135/1825-263X/3319, https://www.researchgate.net/publication/333210572_State_Fragility_Regime_Survival_and_Spoilers_in_South_Sudan

Assal, Munzoul A. M. & Abdul-Jalil, Musa Adam. (2015). Past, present, and future. FIFTY YEARS OF ANTHROPOLOGY IN SUDAN. *Chr. Michelsen Institute. https://www.cmi.no/publications/file/5499-past-present-and-fu-ture.pdf*

Atem, Atem Yaak. Jungle Chronicles and Other Writings: Recollections of a South Sudanese. *Africa World books, 2017.*

Auerbach, M. P. (2021). Global Politics: Causes of War. *Salem Press Encyclopedia.* https://lopes.idm.oclc.org/login?url=https://search.ebscohost.com/login.aspx?direct=true&db=ers&AN=89185503&site=eds-live&scope=site&custid=s8333196&groupid=main&profile=eds1

Awolich, Abraham. (November 25, 2021). Top official from leading think tank in S. Sudan resigns. *Sudan Tribune.* https://sudantribune.com/article226415/?fbclid=IwAR0G72yY-jw12IdMX2asOZiK7jkdBWhTkdreXn1wKAKL5m6vVT7Il-pQlVNXo

Azeez Olaniyan, & Aliyu Yahaya. (2016). Cows, Bandits, and Violent Conflicts: Understanding Cattle Rustling in Northern Nigeria. *Africa Spectrum, 51(3). https://lopes.idm.oclc.org/login?url=https://search.ebscohost.com/login.aspx?direct=true&db=edsdoj&AN=edsdoj.71c943237d794639987c6a22fa5adf7b&site=eds-live&scope=site&custid=s8333196&groupid=main&profile=eds1*

Badal, Raphael Koba. (1977). British Administration in Souther Sudan, 1900-1956: A Study in Colonial Neglect. *ProQuest LLC. https://eprints.soas.ac.uk/29707/1/10752679.pdf*

BBC. (January 16, 2014). Yoweri Museveni: Uganda troops fighting South Sudan rebels. *https://www.bbc.com/news/world-africa-25759650.*

Berkeley, Bill. The Graves Are Not Yet Full: Race, Tribe and Powerin the Heart of Africa. *Basic Books, 2001.*

Berkeley, Bill. (2001). Race, Tribe, and Power in the Heart of Africa. *World Policy Journal, 18(1), 79.* https://search-ebsco-host-com.lopes.idm.oclc.org/login.aspx?direct=true&db=edsjsr&AN=edsjsr.40209734&site=eds-live&scope=site

Berry, L. B. (2015). Sudan, a country study / Federal Research Division, *Library of Congress; edited by LaVerle Berry. Fifth edition.* https://permanent.fdlp.gov/gpo63176/CS_Sudan.pdf#

Brosche, J., & Hoglund, K. (2016). Crisis of governance in South Sudan: electoral politics and violence in the world's newest nation. *Journal of Modern African Studies, 54(1), 67–90.* https://doi-org.lopes.idm.oclc.org/10.1017/S0022278X15000828. https://lopes.idm.oclc.org/login?url=https://search.ebscohost.com/login.aspx?direct=true&db=edswss&AN=000370862400003&site=eds-live&scope=site&custid=s8333196&groupid=-main&profile=eds1

Brownback, Sam (2007). A Remarkable Journey of Faith and Compassion: From Power to Power. *Thomas Nelson*

Churchill, Winston S. The River War: An Account of the Reconquest of the Sudan. *Seven Treasurers Publications, 2008.*

Bruce J Berman. (1998). Ethnicity, Patronage and the African State: The Politics of Uncivil Nationalism. *African Affairs, 97(388), 305.* https://search-ebscohost-com.lopes.idm.oclc.org/login.aspx?direct=true&db=edsjsr&AN=edsjsr.723213&site=eds-live&scope=site

Carolan, G. (2021). Statebuilding in the Peace Agreements of Sudan and South Sudan. *Journal of Intervention & Statebuilding,* *15(1),* *1–24.* *https://lopes.idm.oclc.org/login?url=https://search.ebscohost.com/login.aspx?direct=true&db=edb&AN=148209975&site=edslive&scope=site&custid=s8333196&groupid=main&profile=eds1*

Cline, L. E. (2020). War on the Hoof: regional security in Africa and livestock conflicts. *Small Wars & Insurgencies, 31(1), 87. https://lopes.idm.oclc.org/login?url=https://search.ebscohost.com/login.aspx?direct=true&db=edb&AN=140034439&site=eds-live&scope=site&custid=s8333196&groupid=main&profile=eds1*

Cockett, Richard. Sudan: The Failure and Division of an African State. *Yale Press/New Haven and London, 2010.*

Collins, Roberts O. Land Beyond the Rivers. The Southern Sudan,1898-1918. *New Haven and London, Yale University Press, 1971.*

Collins, Roberts O. The Waters of the Nile: Hydropolitics and the Jonglei Canal, 1900-1988. *Markus Wiener Publishers/Princeton, 1996.*

Collins, Roberts O. The Nile. *Yale University Press/New Haven & London, 2002.*

Constitute. The World's Constitutions to read, search, and compare. South Sudan Constitution (2011), retrieved on November 23, 2021, from

https://www.constituteproject.org/constitution/South_Sudan_2011.pdf

Cormack, Z. (2017). The spectacle of death: visibility and concealment at an unfinished memorial in South Sudan. *Journal of Eastern African Studies, 11(1), 115–132. https:// lopes.idm.oclc.org/login?url=https://search.ebscohost.com/login. aspx?direct=true&db=edb&AN=121549844&site=eds-live&- scope=site&custid=s8333196&groupid=main&profile=eds1*

Dani, Fatiha. (2012). The Growth Nationalism in Sudan under Anglo-Egypt Rule (1899-1956). A Doctoral Thesis for African Civilization. *University of Oran.* https://theses.univ-oran1.dz/document/42201234t.pdf

de Vries, L., & Schomerus, M. (2017). South Sudan's Civil War Will Not End with a Peace Deal. *Peace Review, 29(3), 333.* doi:10.1080/10402659.2017.1344533, https://lopes. idm.oclc.org/login?url=http://search.ebscohost.com/login.as-px?direct=true&db=edb&AN=124637860&site=eds-live&-scope=site

Deng, L. B. (2010). Social capital and civil war: The Dinka communities in Sudan's civil war. *African Affairs, 109(435), 231-250. https://lopes.idm.oclc.org/login?url=https://search. ebscohost.com/login.aspx?direct=true&db=edsjsr&AN=eds-jsr.40785322&site=eds-live&scope=site*

Deng, Francis Mading, forwarded by Kevin M. Cahill, Sudan atthe Brink. *Fordham University Press and the Institute for International Humanitarian Affairs,* New York, 2010.

Deng, Francis Mading. War of Visions, Conflict of Identities inthe Sudan. *The Brooking Institution, Washington D.C, 1995.*

Deng, Francis Mading. Protecting the Dispossessed. A Challengefor the International Community. *The Brooking Institution, Washington D.C, 1993.*

Deng, Lual Achuek. The Power of Creative Reasoning. The Ideas and Vision of John Garang. Bloomington, IN: *iUniverse, Inc., 2013.*

Deng, A. Lual (2020). The National Dialogue: A Framework for Sustainable Peace, Economic Growth, and Poverty Eradication in South Sudan. *Africa World Books. Pty Ldt.*

De Juan, A. (2013). Devolving Ethnic Conflicts: The Role of Subgroup Identities for Institutional Intergroup Settlements. *Civil Wars, 15(1), 78.* https://doi-org.lopes.idm.oclc.org/10.1080/13698249.2013.781304.https://lopes.idm.oclc.org/login?url=https://search.ebscohost.com/login.aspx?direct=true&db=a9h&AN=87373928&site=eds-live&scope=site

de Simone, S. (2018). Playing the 'fragile state' card: the SPLM and state extraversion in South Sudan. *Journal of Modern African Studies, 56(3), 395.*

Dominic Rohner, Mathias Thoenig, & Fabrizio Zilibotti. (2013). Seeds of distrust: Conflict in Uganda. *Journal of Economic Growth, 18(3), 217.* https://doi-org.lopes.idm.oclc.org/10.1007/s10887-013-9093-1. https://lopes.idm.oclc.org/login?url=https://search.ebscohost.com/login.aspx?direct=true&db=edsjsr&AN=edsjsr.42635325&site=eds-live&scope=site

De Waal, A. (2014). When kleptocracy becomes insolvent: brute causes of the civil war in South Sudan. *African Affairs, (452), 347.* https://lopes.idm.oclc.org/login?url=http://search.ebscohost.com/login.aspx?direct=true&db=edsgbc&AN=edsgcl.385345333&site=eds-live&scope=site

Downes, Alexander B. (2006). Desperate Times, Desperate Measures: The Causes of Civilian Victimization in War. *International Security, 30(4), 152–195.* https://lopes.idm.oclc.org/login?url=https://search.ebscohost.com/login.aspx?direct=true&db=edsjsr&AN=edsjsr.4137532&site=eds-live&scope=site

Evans-Pritchard, E.E, edited by John Middleton and DavidTait. Tribes without Rulers, Studies in African SegmentarySystems. *Ruotledge& Kegan Paul Ltd, 1958.*

Evans-Pritchard, E.E. The Nuer: A description of the Modes of Livelihood and Political Institutions of a Nilotic People. *Oxford University Presss, 1940.*

Fardol, Santino. Southern Sudan and Its Flights for Freedom. Bloomington, IN: *AuthorHouse, 2006.*

Garang de Mabior, John, edited and introduced by MansourKhalid, The Call for Democracy in Sudan. *Kegan Paul International Ltd, 1985.*

Ghosh, B. (2010). Birth Pains. *TIME Magazine, 176(13), 40–45.* https://lopes.idm.oclc.org/login?url=https://search.ebscohost.com/login.aspx?direct=true&db=ulh&AN=53787753&site=eds-live&scope=site&custid=s8333196&groupid=main&profile=eds1

Githongo, J. (2006). Inequality, Ethnicity and the Fight against Corruption in Africa: A Kenyan Perspective. *Economic Affairs, 26(4), 19.* https://search-ebscohost-com. lopes.idm.oclc.org/login.aspx?direct=true&db=ed-b&AN=23415199&site=eds-live&scope=site

Hobsawm, E. (2002, February 23). War and peace. *The Guardian.* Retrieved November 22, 2021, from https://www. theguardian.com/education/2002/feb/23/artsandhumanities. highereducation

Hooper, H. D. (1934). Pagan Tribes of the Nilotic Sudan. *InternationalReviewofMission,23*(2),*272–273.*https://search-eb-scohost-com.lopes.idm.oclc.org/login.aspx?direct=true&db=rf-h&AN=ATLAiE58180531001164&site=eds-live&scope=site

Hutchinson, Sharon E. Nuer Dilemmas: Coping with Money,War, and the State. *University of California Press, 1995.*

Hutchinson, Sharon E, & Pendle, Naomi. (2015). Violence, legitimacy, and prophecy: Nuer struggles with uncertainty in South Sudan. *Journal of American Ethnological Society. https:// www.academia.edu/22777271/Violence_legitimacy_and_prophe-cy_Nuer_struggles_with_uncertainty_in_South_Sudan.*

Impey, A. (2013). Keeping in touch via cassette: tracing Dinka songs from cattle camp to transnational audio-letter. *Journal of African Cultural Studies, 25(2), 197–210. https://lopes. idm.oclc.org/login?url=https://search.ebscohost.com/login.aspx?di-rect=true&db=edb&AN=87820879&site=eds-live&scope=site*

Jenkins, Diana (2014). Peace Is More Than the Absence of War. *Huff Post. https://www.huffpost.com/entry/ the-absence-of-war_b_5176243*

Johnson, Dough H. The Upper Nile Province Handbook: AReport on People and Government in the Southern Sudan, 1931 by C.A. Willis, 17. *Oxford University Press, 1995.*

Johnson, Douglas H. Nuer Prophets. A History of Prophecy from the Upper Nile in the Nineteenth and the Twentieth Century.*ClarendonPress.* Oxford, 1994.

Jok, Madut Jok. Sudan: Race, Religion, And Violence. *Oneworld Publications.* Oxford, 2007.

Kane, R. (2014). Ritual Formation of Peaceful Publics: Sacrifice and Syncretism in South Sudan (1991-2005). *Journal of Religion In Africa, 44(3/4), 386-410.*

Khalid, Mansour. Nimeiri and the Revolution of Dis-may. London: Kegan Paul, 1985.

Laws of Southern Sudan, The Child Act 2008. Ministry of Legal Affairs and Constitutional Development. *The Southern Sudan GazetteNo.1 Volume I* , 2009.

Kalpakian, J. V. (2017). Peace agreements in a near-permanent civil war: Learning from Sudan and South Sudan. *South African Journal of International Affairs, 24(1), 1.*

https://lopes.idm.oclc.org/login?url=https://search.ebscohost.com/login.aspx?direct=true&db=edb&AN=123074302&site=eds-live&scope=site&custid=s8333196&groupid=main&profile=eds1

King, R. (2017). Cattle, raiding and disorder in Southern African history. *Africa, 3, 607. https://doi-org.lopes.idm.oclc. org/10.1017/S0001972017000146, https://lopes.idm.oclc.org/ login?url=https://search.ebscohost.com/login.aspx?direct=true&d-b=edsgao&AN=edsgcl.502119681&site=eds-live&scope=site&-custid=s8333196&groupid=main&profile=eds1*

Kostelyanets, S. V. (2021). The Rise and Fall of Political Islam in Sudan. *Politikologija Religije, 15(1), 85–104.* https://lopes.idm.oclc.org/login?url=https://search.eb-scohost.com/login.aspx?direct=true&db=rfh&AN=AT-LAiAZI210510000126&site=eds-live&scope=site&cus-tid=s8333196&groupid=main&profile=eds1

Krause, J. (2019). Stabilization and Local Conflicts: Communal and Civil War in South Sudan. *Ethnopolitics, 18(5), 478–493.* https://lopes.idm.oclc.org/login?url=https:// search.ebscohost.com/login.aspx?direct=true&db=ed-b&AN=137989022&site=eds-live&scope=site&cus-tid=s8333196&groupid=main&profile=eds1

Kuntzelman, C. C. (2013). South Sudan: Solutions for Moving beyond an "Ethnic Conflict." *International Research and Review, 3(1), 81–118.* https://lopes.idm.oclc. org/login?url=https://search.ebscohost.com/login.aspx?di-rect=true&db=eric&AN=EJ1149924&site=eds-live&scope=-site&custid=s8333196&groupid=main&profile=eds1

Lefebvre, Jeffery A. Arms for the Horn. U.S Security Policy inEthiopia and Somalia 1953-1991. *University of Pittsburgh, 199.*

LeRoux-Rutledge, E. (2020). Re-evaluating the "traditional": How the South Sudanese use established gender narratives to advance women's equality and empowerment. *World Development, 132, N.PAG.* https://doi-org.lopes.idm.oclc.org/10.1016/j.worlddev.2020.104929. https://lopes.idm.oclc.org/login?url=https://search.ebscohost.com/login.aspx?direct=true&db=ehh&AN=143419297&site=eds-live&scope=site&custid=s8333196&groupid=main&profile=eds1

Logo MuLukwat, K. H. (2015). Challenges of Regulating Non-International Armed Conflicts - an Examination of Ongoing Trends in South Sudan's Civil War. *Journal of International Humanitarian Legal Studies, 6(2), 414* .

Longar Dau, S. M. A. (2016). On the Discourse and Search for an Appropriate System of Governance: A Case for Ethnic Federalism as a Solution to Ethnic Conflicts and Marginalization in South Sudan. *Global Studies Journal, 9(2), 1.*

Lumumba, Patrick Otieno (JULY 1989). National Security in the Kenyan legal System. A Thesis for the Degree of Master of Laws in the University of Nairobi. *University of Nairobi Research Archive. http://erepository.uonbi.ac.ke/bitstream/handle/11295/11700/Lumumba_National%20security%20in%20the%20Kenyan%20legal%20system.pdf?sequence=1*

Maszka, John (2019). A Strategic Analysis of Conflict in Sudan and South Sudan. *International Affairs and Global Strategy.* https://www.academia.edu/38931570/A_Strategic_Analysis_of_Conflict_in_Sudan_and_South_Sudan

Mawson, A. N. M. (1991). "Bringing What People Want": Shrine Politics among the Agar Dinka. *Africa (Edinburgh University Press), 61(3), 354–369. https://doi-org.lopes.idm. oclc.org/10.2307/1160030, https://lopes.idm.oclc.org/login?url=https://search.ebscohost.com/login.aspx?direct=true&db=rlh&AN=11675250&site=eds-live&scope=site*

Mawut, Lazarus Leek (1995). The Southern Sudan under British Rule 1898-1924: the constraints reassessed. *Durham theses, Durham University*. Available at Durham E-Theses Online: http://etheses.dur.ac.uk/971/

McFerson, Hazel M. (2009). Governance and Hyper-Corruption in Resource-Rich African Countries. *Third World Quarterly, 30(8), 1529–1547*. https://doi-org.lopes.idm.oclc.org/10.1080/01436590903279257

Modi, L. P., Opongo, E. O., & Smith, R. D. (2019). South Sudan's Costly Conflict and the Urgent Role of Religious Leaders. *The Review of Faith & International Affairs, 17(2), 37–46*. https://doi-org.lopes.idm.oclc.org/10.1080/15570274.2019.1608660. https://lopes.idm.oclc.org/login?url=https://search.ebscohost.com/login.aspx?direct=true&db=rfh&AN=ATLAiA14190617000293&site=eds-live&scope=site&custid=s8333196&groupid=main&profile=eds1

Morris, Nsamba Adam. (2011). State Building and Development in South Sudan. *African Research and Resource Forum*. https://www.academia.edu/26585030/State_Building_and_Development_in_South_Sudan

Mutanda, D. (2019). The Centrality of Conflict Transformation in Solving Political Struggles and Political Violence in South Sudan. *Strategic Review for Southern Africa, 41(1).* https://lopes.idm.oclc.org/login?url=https://search.ebscohost.com/login.aspx?direct=true&db=eds-gao&AN=edsgcl.602243269&site=eds-live&scope=site&custid=s8333196&groupid=main&profile=eds1

Nasredeen, A. (2013). Identities and citizenship in Sudan: Governing constitutional principles. *African Human Rights Law Journal, (2), 383.* https://lopes.idm.oclc.org/login?url=http://search.ebscohost.com/login.aspx?direct=true&db=edssci&AN=edssci.S1996.20962013000200007&site=eds-live&scope=site

Nyaba, Peter Adwok. The Politics of Liberation in South Sudan: An Insider's View. Kampala: *Fountain Publishers, 1997.*

Nyaba, Peter Adwok. South Sudan: The State We Aspire To. Wanneroo, Australia: *Africa World Books pty Ltd, second Edition, 2016.*

O'Fahey, R. S. (1996). Islam and Ethnicity in the Sudan. *Journal of Religion in Africa, 26(3),* 258–267. https://lopes.idm.oclc.org/login?url=https://search.ebscohost.com/login.aspx?direct=true&db=rfh&AN=ATLA0001015901&site=eds-live&scope=site&custid=s8333196&groupid=main&profile=eds1

Okeke, Remi Chukwudi., Idike, Adeline Nnenna., Akwara, Azalahu Francis., Korie, Cornelius O., & Ibiam, Okechukwu E. (2021). Failure of States, Fragility of States, and the Prospects of Peace in South Sudan. *SAGE Open, 11.* https://doi-org.lopes.idm.oclc.org/10.1177/21582440211020483

Omer, R. (2016). South Sudan: from independence to a detrimental civil war. *Harvard International Review, (3),* *11.* https://lopes.idm.oclc.org/login?url=http://search.ebscohost.com/login.aspx?direct=true&db=edsgao&AN=edsgcl.459804754&site=eds-live&scope=site

Pearson, A. L., & Muchunguzi, C. (2011). Contextualizing Privatization and Conservation in the History of Resource Management in Southwestern Uganda: Ethnicity, Political Privilege, and Resource Access over Time. *International Journal of African Historical Studies, 44(1), 113–140.* https://search-ebscohost-com.lopes.idm.oclc.org/login.aspx?direct=true&db=ofs&AN=510058834&site=eds-live&scope=site

Pendle, N. R. (2020). Politics, prophets, and armed mobilizations: competition and continuity over registers of authority in South Sudan's conflicts. *Journal of Eastern African Studies, 14(1),* *43–62.* https://doi-org.lopes.idm.oclc.org/10.1080/17531055.2019.1708545. https://lopes.idm.oclc.org/login?url=https://search.ebscohost.com/login.aspx?direct=true&db=edswss&AN=000506324700001&site=eds-live&scope=site&custid=s8333196&groupid=main&profile=eds1

Pinaud, C. (2014). South Sudan: civil war, predation and the making of a military aristocracy. *African Affairs, (451),* *192.* https://lopes.idm.oclc.org/login?url=http://search.ebscohost.com/login.aspx?direct=true&db=edsgao&AN=edsgcl.374368814&site=eds-live&scope=site

Pospisil, J. (2014). Civil War in South Sudan: Bloody Ethno-Politics and a Failed International Engagement. (PolicyPaper / Österreichisches Institut für Internationale Politik, 3). Wien: *Österreichisches Institut für Internationale Politik (oiip)*. https://nbn-resolving.org/urn:nbn:de:0168-ssoar-58638-1.

Radon, J., & Logan, S. (2014). South Sudan: Governance arrangements, war, and peace. *Journal of International Affairs, (1), 149.* https://lopes.idm.oclc.org/login?url=http://search.ebscohost.com/login.aspx?direct=true&db=edsgao&AN=edsgcl.396527047&site=eds-live&scope=site

Raftopoulos, Brian, & Alexander, Karin. (2006). Peace in the Balance: The Crisis in Sudan. *Journal of Eastern African Studies. Institute for Justice and Reconciliation.* http://african-minds.co.za/wp-content/uploads/2012/05/Peace%20in%20the%20Balance%20-%20The%20Crisis%20in%20Sudan.pdf

Rolandsen, Øystein H. (2015) Another civil war in South Sudan: the failure of Guerrilla Government? *Journal of Eastern African Studies 9(1):163-174,* DOI:10.1080/17531055.2014.993210.

Sano, K. (2019). "One" but Divided: Tribalism and Grouping among Secondary School Students in South Sudan. *Anthropology & Education Quarterly, 50(2), 189–204.*

Schake, K. (2017). What Causes War? *Orbis, 61(4), 449–462.* https://doi-org.lopes.idm.oclc.org/10.1016/j.orbis.2017.08.002, https://lopes.idm.oclc.org/login?url=https://search.ebscohost.com/login.aspx?direct=true&db=edselp&AN=S0030438717300698&site=eds-live&scope=site&custid=s8333196&groupid=main&profile=eds1

Schouten, P., & Bachmann, J. (2020). Buffering State-making: Geopolitics in the Sudd Marshlands of South Sudan. *GEOPOLITICS*. https://doi-org.lopes.idm.oclc.org/10.1080/14650045.2020.1858283,

Shaffer, Ryan. 2021. "South Sudan: The Untold Story from Independence to Civil War." *TERRORISM AND POLITICAL VIOLENCE 33 (7): 1581–85.* doi:10.1080/09546553.2021.1976551, https://lopes.idm.oclc.org/login?url=https://search.ebscohost.com/login.aspx?direct=true&db=edswss&AN=000705040800017&site=eds-live&scope=site&custid=s8333196&groupid=main&profile=eds1

Singer, P.W, edited by Robert J. Art, Robert Jervis, Stephen J. Walt. Corporate Warriors, The Rise of the Privatized Military Industry. *Cornell Press, Ithaca and London, 2008.*

Spittaels, Steven, & Weyns, Yannick. (2014). Mapping Conflict Motives: the Sudan - South Sudan Border. *Academia Letters.* https://www.academia.edu/10372816/Mapping_Conflict_Motives_the_Sudan_South_Sudan_Border

Suliman, Mohamed (1997). Civil War in Sudan: The Impact of Ecological Degradation, Contributions in Black Studies. *A Journal of African and Afro-American Studies, Vol. 15*(7). https://scholarworks.umass.edu/cibs/vol15/iss1/7

Sweeney, M. S. (2016). The spoiling of the world: in South Sudan decades of civil war led to independence--and yet more war. MHQ: *The Quarterly Journal of Military History, (1). 76.* https://lopes.idm.oclc.org/login?url=http://search.ebscohost.com/login.aspx?direct=true&db=edsgao&AN=edsgcl.459722102&site=eds-live&scope=site

(2013). South Sudan slides towards civil war despite international efforts. *Al-Arab (London, United Kingdom).* https://lopes.idm.oclc.org/login?url=http://search.ebscohost.com/login.aspx?direct=true&db=edsgin&AN=edsgcl.353745539&site=eds-live&scope=site

(2016). Fears of civil war grow as fighting shakes South Sudan; Factions clash in capital Juba with gunfire striking UN compound sheltering 25,000. *The Toronto Star (Toronto, Ontario).* https://lopes.idm.oclc.org/login?url=http://search.ebscohost.com/login.aspx?direct=true&db=edsgin&AN=edsgcl.457465002&site=eds-live&scope=site

(2017). Millions flee civil war in South Sudan; Fears of potential genocide mount. *Cape Times (South Africa).* https://lopes.idm.oclc.org/login?url=http://search.ebscohost.com/login.aspx?direct=true&db=edsgin&AN=edsgcl.495805877&site=eds-live&scope=site

Taylor & Francis. Conflict and impasse in South Sudan. (2017). *Strategic Comments, 23(4), i–ii.* https://lopes.idm.oclc.org/login?url=https://search.ebscohost.com/login.aspx?direct=true&db=edb&AN=123226392&site=eds-live&scope=site&custid=s8333196&groupid=main&profile=eds1

Tekalign, Yohannes. (2015). Challenges for Peace in South Sudan: Problems and opportunities of solving the current civil war. *International Researchers (4)2,* https://www.academia.edu/14186302/CHALLENGES_FOR_PEACE_IN_SOUTH_SUDAN_PROBLEMS_AND_OPPORTUNITIES_OF_SOLVING_THE_CURRENT_CIVIL_WAR

Tepfenhart, M. (2013). The Causes of Ethnic Conflicts. *Comparative Civilizations Review, 68, 84–97.* https://lopes. idm.oclc.org/login?url=https://search.ebscohost.com/login. aspx?direct=true&db=ofs&AN=87591213&site=eds-live&-scope=site&custid=s8333196&groupid=main&profile=eds1

(2017). South Sudan's sacked army chief quits Juba, dismisses fears amid civil war. *Times of Oman (Muscat, Oman).* https://lopes.idm.oclc.org/login?url=http://search.ebsco-host.com/login.aspx?direct=true&db=edsgin&AN=eds-gcl.496364035&site=eds-live&scope=site

The Citizen (Dar Es Salaam, Tanzania) - AAGM. (2020). Exposing South Sudan governance failure. https:// lopes.idm.oclc.org/login?url=https://search.ebscohost. com/login.aspx?direct=true&db=edsgao&AN=eds-gcl.640096905&site=eds-live&scope=site&cus-tid=s8333196&groupid=main&profile=eds1

The Fund for Peace. (2021). Measuring Fragility Risk and Vulnerability

in 179 Countries. *Fragile States Index.* https://fragilestatesin-dex.org/

The Shutterstock Editorial. (2017). Child Brides, Rumbek, South Sudan. https://www.shutterstock.com/editorial/image-editorial/child-brides-rumbek-south-sudan-31-jul-2017-9029312b

Trouwborst, A. A. (1973). The Azande. History and political institutions E. E. Evans-Pritchard. *Bijdragen Tot de Taal-, Land- EnVolkenkunde, 129(1), 157.* https://search-ebscohost-com.lopes.idm.oclc.org/login.aspx?direct=true&db=edsjsr&AN=edsjsr.27861317&site=eds-live&scope=site

Van De Kerkhof, Marlie, Mathijs Van Leeuwen, and Yves Van Leynseele. 2018. "Transforming Land Governance and Strengthening the State in South Sudan." *African Affairs 117 (467): 286–309.* https://search-ebscohost-com.lopes.idm.oclc.org/login.aspx?direct=true&db=edb&AN=129289279&site=eds-live&scope=site

Young, J. (2003). Sudan: Liberation Movements, Regional Armies, Ethnic Militias & Peace. *Review of African Political Economy, 30 (97),* 423–434. https://lopes.idm.oclc.org/login?url=https://search.ebscohost.com/login.aspx?direct=true&db=edb&AN=11936325&site=eds-live&scope=site&custid=s8333196&groupid=main&profile=eds1

INDEX

Jok, Madut Jok. 28, 104, 116, 188
Jomo 145
Jon 156
Jonglei 32, 46, 51-3, 70-2, 75, 95-6, 99, 134, 156, 183
Joseph 47, 115, 124-6
Joshua 51, 53
Juba 15, 31, 43, 51, 53, 56, 61, 64-5, 70-1, 73, 75, 79, 81, 92, 95, 103, 107, 112-4, 148, 165, 196-7
Juma 104
Kageme 131
Kalpakian, J. 188
Kane, R. 138, 188
Kanjai 104
Karin 4, 34-5, 194
Kegan 128, 186, 188
Kenya 145
Kenyan 63, 187, 190
Kerkhof 152-153, 198
Kerubino 113
Ket 104
Kevin 44, 147, 184
Khalid, Mansour. 128, 188
Kharotum 18, 38, 41, 90, 118

Khartoum 11, 30, 39, 42-3, 51, 54, 57, 82-3, 89-90, 95, 102-3, 112, 127, 140
Khartuom 139
Khor 50, 70
Khorfuluth 72
Kiir 14, 28, 36, 56, 58-9, 62, 67, 73, 75, 79, 91, 100-4, 110-4, 117, 124-6, 132-3, 139, 142, 147, 159
Kiwawulo 125-126
Koba 50, 181
Kok 104
Kong 89, 101
Kongor 80-81, 86
Korie 192
Kostelyanets, S. 172, 189
Koyor 104
Krause, J. 134, 189
Kuai 104
Kueth 156
Kuir 104
Kuntzelman, C. 14, 189
Kuthin 104
Kuwa 31
Lady 171
Lagu 47, 126-8
Laka 81